HEALTH AND HEALING

PASTORAL CARE AND ETHICAL ISSUES

HEALTH AND HEALING
A Ministry to Wholeness

Denis Duncan

THE SAINT ANDREW PRESS
· EDINBURGH ·

First published in 1988 by
THE SAINT ANDREW PRESS
121 George Street, Edinburgh EH2 4YN

Copyright © Denis Duncan 1988

ISBN 0 7152 0615 X

British Library Cataloguing in Publication Data
Duncan, Denis
Health and healing.
1. Christian Church. Ministry of healing
I. Title   II. Series
265′.82

ISBN 0–7152–0615–X

All biblical references from RSV unless otherwise stated.

Printed in Great Britain by
Billing & Sons Ltd, Worcester

Contents

Introduction

It was in 1957 that I made my way one Thursday afternoon from my manse in the East End of Glasgow to a small sanctuary in the Gorbals district of that city. I had asked Cameron Peddie, then a parish minister in that famous area just south of the river—the 'old' Gorbals, which was then associated in the public mind with gangs and slums and extensive social deprivation—if I could come to his healing sanctuary and observe his ministry in action. He immediately and graciously said that I would be very welcome to do so, and we arranged an appropriate date.

I was at the time the minister of Trinity-Duke Street Parish Church in Dennistoun, having gone there after my first ministry in St Margaret's Parish Church, Juniper Green in Edinburgh. My East End parish was, perhaps surprisingly, much more representative of social groups and backgrounds than suburban Edinburgh where my church then was, in the late 1940s, very much the 'village church'. The suburban population tended to become members of 'the other church', Saint Andrew's Parish Church, famous for its great sequence of ministers—Norman Macfarlane, George S Gunn and George T H Reid. My parish in Dennistoun, in Glasgow, although it included such institutions as The Cattle Market (shades of Nineveh—'... and much cattle'), Tennants' Brewery and Duke Street Prison (not technically within my parish, but just down the road), had many members of the professions not only from residential Dennistoun (our manse was one of at least 15 within a square mile, known perhaps not surprisingly as 'Mount Zion'), but also from sections of the Gallowgate and downwards towards Bridgeton.

I found myself more and more concerned about the kind of pastoral ministry required in such situations. This led to

7

my involvement with the Davidson Clinic, possibly the first psychotherapeutically orientated counselling centre in the United Kingdom (the other centre, the first of the two in Scotland, was in Edinburgh), and the approach to pastoral care which that involved. It also made me aware of 'the forgotten talent', the healing ministry as expressed by Cameron Peddie whose moving and indeed mighty statement about the need for the recovery of the healing ministry was expressed in his famous book under that title. In *The Forgotten Talent*[1] he recorded the reasons for his returning, in the second half of his ministry, as it were, to, as he saw it, essential Christianity expressed in Christ's dual but distinctive command to the disciples: 'Preach as you go, saying, "The kingdom of heaven is at hand." Heal the sick ...' (Matt 10: 7–8).

Cameron Peddie's record of his recovering the forgotten talent is exciting. It is the story of a man, often described as 'the Saint of the Gorbals', who came to his parish determined to proclaim and practise the 'social' Gospel and, while not for one moment dismissing the importance of working at and with the social problems and 'incarnating' the Gospel in such a ministry, began to see that there was a dimension that was missing in his ministry. It was that which compelled him to go back to the very foundations of his faith and to realise that the missing dimension involved the forgotten talent—the Christian ministry of healing.

If I call the dimension that had to be recovered and brought into ministry at the parish and practical level 'the spiritual dimension', I will offend those who—wholly properly and rightly—say that caring love, where given in Jesus' name, without thought of return, is also a 'spiritual' activity—it is. What I mean by 'the spiritual dimension' in this discussion is my belief that there are raised levels of awareness in which we 'touch and handle things unseen'[2] in such a way that insight is given and internal inspiration (which represents 'growth' in the spiritual aspect of our being) is conveyed so that our perspective on life is considerably changed. I have said elsewhere that the Christian stance must be governed by St Paul's great statement in 1 Corinthians about true reality.[3] It is 'the things which are seen that are temporal and the things which are not seen that are eternal'. Reality is not what we see, touch and feel, but is of another kind and is summed up for St Paul by the word 'eternal'. The raised level of awareness is dramatically illustrated in the story of the walk to Emmaus (to which I shall return). The knowledge gained in such a situation is the knowledge which 'is beyond knowledge' described by St Paul in his most glorious statement in Ephesians chapter 3.[4] It is not the everyday knowledge with which our minds are concerned and which is of a rational, intellectual nature and at the purely mental level. It is a 'spiritual' knowledge that comes through intuition and imagination and which is revealed through the prompting of the Holy Spirit.

The healing ministry, as I met it in Cameron Peddie's sanctuary that Thursday afternoon, was an expression of that spiritual dimension in action. It was the product of a year of preparation—and it took a year of 'waiting on God' to determine whether Cameron Peddie should enter into the healing ministry at all. Once it had begun it was sustained by 'the hour of watch'—from 11pm to midnight each night. Because it is a ministry so related to the activity of the Holy Spirit, without whose presence and power nothing can be done,[5] it is a ministry that must be encompassed in prayer. I shall say more of that later.

The experience of the mystic is not given (and it can only be *given*) to many. St Paul was taken to the 'third heaven'[6] and saw wonders there. My friend and colleague, the Revd Dr Martin Israel, pathologist and priest, is undoubtedly one of that very special and limited company. Cameron Peddie, because of his profound devotional life and his developed relationship with Christ, was another.

The trauma that hit me on that first visit to the sanctuary was compounded by the manifest evidence of the height, and depth, of the spiritual life of this Gorbals saint—a word appropriate to him in the true Reformation sense, as to us all, but accurate in another sense (which he would wholly deny) far beyond the reach of most of us. I had gone to observe and to ponder. I had no theology of this ministry or theory about it—I was there to learn. Suddenly without any warning whatsoever, Cameron Peddie said to me, 'Denis, would you take some of those waiting? There are too many for me today'. There was no escape. I had listened to what he said to those

receiving ministry. 'Do you feel warmth?' 'Do you feel cold?'
I had become aware that he laid hands on, as he called it
later in conversation, 'the affected part'. What I 'heard'
him saying in asking me to do this was that, by virtue of
ordination or more likely 'membership of the church, the
healing community' (as he did not confine participation to
ordained ministers), we are all called to healing ministry 'in
Jesus' name'. That he himself was so much further along the
spiritual path was not, in his view relevant, or so it seemed,
although it felt overwhelmingly relevant to me. He seemed
also to be saying that this was the church's ministry and was
not confined to certain individuals with healing gifts. The
experience was traumatic, but it was my entry to the ministry
of healing.

That was 30 years ago, so it is from the perspective of those
years that I will try to give some picture of the ministry of
healing today. The small group of us then involved in the
healing ministry were very much on the fringe of the church
and perhaps thought by many to be eccentric (which means
what it says—ec-centric. This is from the Greek *ek* and *kentron*
meaning 'away from the centre'.) Now we live in times when
this ministry has been recovered in the churches to an extent
I would not have believed possible three decades ago. The
healing ministry is not yet—perhaps can never be, as it should
be—a normal and essential part of the life, work and witness
of every congregation or parish. It has however moved a long
way in that direction.
   I shall try, in this book, to make readers feel something
of the excitement that has been generated by the recovery
of the ministry of healing in the churches and beyond them.
It is a growth point in the deepest spiritual sense. I shall
interpret phrases like 'the healing ministry', 'the ministry
of healing', and so on, in a much wider sense than may
be expected by those who are uneasy with public dramatic
and emotional expressions of the ministry which are assumed
by many to be the healing ministry in its totality—they
are not. Much suspicion of the ministry, does, however,
derive from its being associated only with that kind of
ministry.

I will try to expand on this ministry in a way helpful to the 'thinking layman or woman', but I hope I can interest the clergy also in this concept of ministry.

I shall place major emphasis on the perennial problem of suffering about which so many in the extensive and varied field of healing generally seem too glib. I shall want to give considerable prominence to the concept of the church as 'the healing community' and spell out some of the implications of that principle.

I believe that while there is a proper and admirable simple faith, illness is often over-simplified. I shall want to look at some of the factors that make it both complex and complicated. This will involve us in consideration of both psychotherapeutic and charismatic approaches to 'the healing of the memories'. I hope to be able to offer some comment on aids to worship, devotion and the development of the spiritual life of which, I believe, meditation is one.

I will discuss both the meaning of health and attempt a definition of that elusive concept, but I have decided not to start there. I have never been part of a committee or working party on health and healing that did not begin with an attempt to define health—and took an excessively long time to do so, without definitive results. Therefore I have tended to find that area a trifle wearisome and unproductive. So, I will place this discussion towards the middle of the book and hope the excitement felt over developments in this field will create the energy needed to wrestle with definitions of health and carry the reader on to further creative aspects of the ministry of healing.

I will allude to some of the difficulties in the field of health and healing towards the end of the book and finish by setting out a fairly extensive list of resources in terms of literature, cassettes and video in this expanding field.

There are two other areas on which I will touch. One is the necessary reminder that the ministry of healing must never be confined to *individual* healing—whatever that means is still to be explained, but it is the word individual that I stress here—but must be related to *corporate* aspects of healing.[7] I expect the ministry of healing to go deeply in to this area in the next decade. I will also, although I am not a professional theologian but simply one who has had to learn theology in the busy market place and high street in which my ministries have been expressed, refer to the theology of healing. I cannot however deal with the theme of health, healing and wholeness without expressing my belief that a theology of healing has not yet been properly established, and that there is much work to be done in that area in days to come—and I mean nearer, not more distant, days.

This book has been written against a background of work pressure arising from the demands of ministry in the various forms in which I am called to express it. It will inevitably lack the care and tidiness demanded by academic writing and will not therefore meet needs of that kind. It is however written with enthusiasm and even passion for the extension of the ministry of healing, as a normal part of the work of our Lord's church today. It seeks to be a balanced presentation of that ministry that, at the same time, conveys something of the thrill of involvement in trying to be obedient to Jesus' command.

I hope something of that excitement is conveyed in this exposition of the healing way.

Notes to Introduction

1   Cameron Peddie, *The Forgotten Talent* (first published by Fontana, 1966. Now published in a new edition by Arthur James, 1985.)
2   A phrase from Horatius Bonar's hymn, 'Here, O my Lord, I see Thee face to face'.
3   Denis Duncan, *Creative Silence* (Arthur James, 1980)
4   Ephesians 3:19, *New English Bible*
5   Acts 4:31
6   II Corinthians 12:2
7   An important book in relation to 'corporate aspects of healing' is *Community, Church and Healing* by R A Lambourne, (first published by Darton, Longman and Todd Ltd in 1963. Now published in a new edition by Arthur James, 1987).

1

A Ministry Recovered

The 1980s have been years of excitement so far as health and healing are concerned, but I leave the discussion of the concept of health until later. What I want to convey, at the very beginning of this study, is a sense of exhilaration and enthusiasm over the recovery of the importance of the ministry of healing in our times.

This is not the place to present a history of the church's attitude to healing ministry or its practice—or indeed lack of practice. Morton Kelsey has fulfilled that major task superbly in his book, *Healing and Christianity*.[1] He writes of the decline in the practice of Christian healing from the fourth century on and shows how it has been a minor concern for long periods in the church's life. That Cameron Peddie, in the 1950s, should call his book *The Forgotten Talent* points to his sense of the failure in the church in this matter.[2] The way in which the recovery of the healing ministry has evolved in the late 1980s is something so significant that it must be 'a straw in the wind of the Spirit'.

I shall discuss at some length the main elements in this extraordinary evolution later. I first want to underline why the word *recovery* is important.

There is always a danger that the church, when under severe pressure in relation to loss of members and influence, will be tempted to lower its standards and turn to gimmicks in order to attract attention. Such a policy is doomed to failure when looked at in spiritual terms. Christianity has always lost influence when it has set out to be popular and acceptable. Its strength has often been demonstrated in the commitment of both individuals and 'remnants' (that glorious Old Testament concept) and the dedication of minorities. 'What is it to you? Follow me' said Jesus to Peter.[3] This is a call to personal

13

obedience as well as an instruction to look after one's own level of discipleship instead of making judgments on others. Obedience, moreover, often leads to the need to be not conformist but *non*-conformist. If Christianity is to be attractive, paradoxically it has to be demanding. The church is most likely to grow when it is true to itself and asks a great deal of its disciples.

Certain aspects of transatlantic Christianity confirm, in very unattractive ways, the danger of gimmicks, the superficiality of techniques as a road to the Kingdom, and the disaster that can follow when the things of the Spirit are abused by being trivialised. The warning given by Peter to Simon Magus in the Acts of the Apostles about demeaning the Holy Spirit and His gifts—including that of the ability to produce signs and wonders and miraculous healings[4] —is a cautionary tale and needs to be heeded by those attracted to the healing ministry today.

Because there has been such a revival of interest in the healing ministry in our day, because it is often demonstrated that where churches take the healing ministry seriously, because the ministry of healing is one of the manifest growth points in the church, the danger of a band-wagon effect is all too possible. As an awareness of the new emphasis on healing ministry comes into consciousness, so there will be a temptation for people to jump on that healing band-wagon. It is therefore necessary to lay down three basic principles for all, individuals and congregations, who would feel drawn to involve themselves in this ministry in order to safeguard it. These three principles are as follows:

1   The healing ministry must be encompassed in prayer.
2   The healing ministry must be built, founded and grounded in the Word of God, the supreme rule of faith and life.
3   The development of the healing ministry must be a subject for constant reflection under the guidance of the Holy Spirit.

Let me briefly develop these three principles:

1   Encompassed in Prayer

In the fourth chapter of the Acts of the Apostles,[5] there is the story of a remarkable miracle carried out by the apostles. This chapter is a gold-mine for the understanding of the church's healing ministry, and I shall return to it at various times. What it contains that is relevant to this first and basic principle is the statement that 'they were all filled with the Holy Spirit'.[6]

The disciples had just made their plea in the prayer they offered in the face of a command not to speak 'in the name of Jesus'. They had asked for the power to speak the Word with boldness and they had prayed that God would confirm that spoken word by demonstrating signs and wonders. The link between the discipleship that involves proclamation and the power that confirms the Word *is* prayer. The Spirit comes in response to prayer.

Two practical points arise out of this. *First*, within the Christian healing ministry, we do not speak of ourselves as 'healers', for it is not in our power to work the miracles of grace. We see ourselves as part of the church, the healing community, as, simply, channels of God's power. We still see ourselves, of course, as totally unworthy to be used in this way, and that feeling is proper and right, for it is the feeling that great servants of the Lord have always experienced—Isaiah, conscious of both personal and corporate unworthiness,[7] Moses throwing off his shoes before the awe-full holiness of God,[8] Paul, 'the foremost of sinners'.[9] It is indeed an essential part of authentic discipleship. Without such a sense of unworthiness and the attitude of humility that it engenders, we cannot be channels at all.

The fact that the efficacy of a sacrament is not dependent on the worth and therefore the holiness of the one who dispenses it is a principle of enormous comfort. It is one that applies in the healing ministry. God's power is made perfect in our weakness.[10] (This is not, incidentally, an excuse for avoiding the struggle, with the help of grace, towards sanctification. It is simply a statement of the truth about our continuing lack of sanctification. It is necessary to be aware of that gap between what we are and what we ought to be if we are to involve ourselves, as part of the healing community, in this ministry. The ministry of healing and spiritual arrogance cannot live together.)

The *second* practical necessity is the provision of means of grace that help us to make real the link between power and prayer. I will deal with this in a later chapter.

2   Founded on Biblical Authority

There may be some differences in the understanding of authority in different denominations. Some will place more emphasis on tradition. Some may simply make the *verba ipsissima* of Jesus the only authority. It is the words of Jesus himself that they feel to be important, rather than the authority of a book. None of these variations affects the essential point which I seek to make in this context, and that is that the way in which we carry out the healing ministry in Christ's name must not be based on our subjective feelings and attitudes. There must be an objective standard, and a testing-point against which we assess all that we do. That objective standard is the record of Jesus' ministry and the early church's understanding of it as contained in the Scriptures; Scriptures that must never be interpreted in a literalist way, but rather in terms of sound Reformed practice, namely that they are read and understood, only under the guidance and influence of the Spirit. It is only as the Holy Spirit illumines the page that insight comes and understanding is forwarded. It is that kind of authority that must determine our understanding of the healing ministry.

3   Reflected On, Under the Spirit

This point, in effect, follows on from the first two, but it is made in this extra way to stress the need for ongoing engagement in prayer and continuing study of the Word in order to know the will of God. In other words, the further development of the healing ministry can only properly be effected if it is the product of the discernment of God's will, not if it comes from our vain imaginings, fantasy, imagination and wishful thinking. 'Thy will be done' must be, and remain, the fundamental desire of the church,—the healing community. To substitute superficial gimmickry for obedience and commitment is indeed '[to] crucify to themselves the Son of God afresh, and put him to an open shame'.[11]

Why then is the word *recovered* so crucial? It is simply because in emphasising the healing ministry, in talking of the *forgotten* talent, the church is going back to its roots in the

New Testament. It is returning to that 'essential Christianity', to which I have already referred.' It is in the light of this that we must go back to Acts chapter 4.

I have pointed out already that the prayer the apostles offered in their predicament, in relation to the authorities who had freed them on the understanding that they must not speak, preach or evangelise 'in the name of Jesus', was crucially important. It bound together proclamation and healing. I quote the crucial words:

> 'And now, Lord, behold their threatenings: and grant unto thy servants, that with all boldness they may speak thy word, By stretching forth thine hand to heal; and that signs and wonders may be done by the name of thy holy child Jesus.
> Acts 4:29–30, Authorised Version

In this holding together of preaching the Word and practising the Word, they were reflecting the first instruction that they had been given when they were commissioned by Jesus to preach and heal.[12]

This command to the disciples enshrines the two tasks of discipleship—then and now—as the declaration in words of the Good News, and a demonstration in action of the content of its message; that, in Jesus, the power of the Kingdom is present, and that men and women can be made whole through him, that he is 'the way, and the truth, and the life';[13] that coming to him, the weary will find rest;[14] that believing in him, accepting from him and committing oneself to him, leads to life.

The miracles are signs that the power of the Kingdom is present.[15]

Jesus' ministry then was proclamation, but it was also the Gospel in action. To preach the word with boldness (note the number of times the word *boldness* occurs in Acts 4) is one side of the coin. The love of God for his people and his desire to bring them into a right relationship with him through repentance, forgiveness, acceptance and grace is the other side of that coin. It is the divine compassion in action.

The offering of that love in compassion leads to the miracles of healing, the feeding of the 5000, the words of comfort offered to a woman taken in adultery,[16] as to a woman of bad reputation whose love in action will be forever proclaimed as part of the Gospel.[17]

So the disciples were called to preach the Gospel and to demonstrate it in action. The church can only be the church when it is, in its obedience, doing these things too. It is the growing consciousness of an historic deficiency in relation to the second instruction that has led, primarily, to the recovery of the healing ministry in our time.

The renewal of interest in the healing ministry has been a feature of virtually all the churches. It has been expressed in various ways, one of the most significant being the appointment in several branches of the church of advisers on health and healing.

The first appointment in this field was that of Bishop Morris Maddocks, then Bishop of Selby, to be Adviser to the Archbishops of Canterbury and York on health and healing. Bishop Maddocks had long been recognised as a leader in the field of Christian healing ministry and had given a great deal of time to forwarding its recovery. In 1981, his study of *The Christian Healing Ministry* was published[18] and it has become a standard guide on that ministry. He followed this with two paperbacks, *Christian Adventure*[19] and *Journey to Wholeness*,[20] and has recently published *A Healing House of Prayer*[21] based on Leslie Weatherhead's famous classic *A Private House of Prayer*.[22] This book is the product of his particular concern with prayer as the essential element in relation to this ministry. His appointment has had a major effect in the Church of England and will continue to do so through the organisation which he has set up, the *Acorn Healing Trust*.[23] In the context of this chapter, the significant element is the Archbishops' decision to allow one of their bishops to express his ministry in a full-time commitment to forwarding the recovery of the church's ministry of healing in the Anglican Communion and indeed beyond it. Bishop Maddocks has been involved in conferences, teaching and listening in many branches of the church.

The United Reformed Church has taken a similar step. This statistically small denomination,[24] has had an influence far beyond its size in the recovery of the healing ministry. It

has produced a great deal of literature helpful to those pursu-
ing every aspect of the healing ministry and it has provided
probably the most valuable single kit related to this subject. It
is called *Health and Healing: a study kit*,[25] and brings together a
large selection of helpful and practical material of great value
to those beginning to think of the possibility of introducing
the ministry to their own congregation or indeed extending
existing ministry.

One of those primarily responsible for the contribution of
the United Reformed Church is now Adviser to that church
on health and healing. He is the Revd David Dale, Moderator
of the General Assembly of the United Reformed Church
(1986–87) and presently Chairman of The Churches' Council
for Health and Healing. He was appointed Adviser in 1985.

The Methodist Church also took a similar step in 1984.
The Revd Howard Booth, one of its senior superintendent
ministers, was given the same advisory role in that church,
spending most of his time and ministry on this task.

Other denominations—for instance, my own, the Church
of Scotland—set up committees to study this ministry while
in, for example, the Baptist Union of Great Britain and
Ireland, the annual conference of its Health and Healing
Group has grown from the small group which I addressed
nearly a decade ago meeting in one room, to an annual
gathering attended by around 150 people. Other churches—
the Presbyterian Church in Ireland for example, which was in
the vanguard of those concerned with, as it was usually called
there, Divine Healing—have continued to develop their work
and witness.

It would be impossible to set out, except in a statistical and
factual way that would be boring, the extent of the change in
the churches in the 1980s—to which the major appointments
that I have mentioned all belong. It may be sufficient to say
that The Churches' Council for Health and Healing[26] (which
embraces all the major denominations—some 23 at the time
of writing—has observers from the Roman Catholic and
Pentecostal Churches, has representative members from
the Royal Colleges of Medicine and Nursing, and from the
British Medical Association (BMA); representatives of healing
fellowships, guilds and associations[27] and has representatives

from the hospital chaplaincies). It has had to abandon what seemed a possible aim in the early 1980s—to be aware of all healing services, agencies, homes, and so on, in the country for resources purposes simply because it is impossible to know or cope with the vast number of, for example, healing services now taking place. Whereas ten years ago one might have had to search for a service which offered ministry by the laying on of hands, they are now numerous.

The healing ministry has not yet been seen, in every denomination or by all churches, to be a normal part of the life, work and witness of a congregation or parish, as it should be in terms of our understanding of essential Christianity, but it has moved an immense distance in that direction.

It is this kind of widespread, cross–denominational effort to make this ministry a normal part of the life of the church that leads me to describe it as a 'straw in the wind of the Spirit'. This is not to deny that there are still many, clergy and lay, who are suspicious of or anxious about the healing ministry. Often, that anxiety is associated with experience of or hearsay about public, emotional and dramatic occasions where an evangelist, or one who calls himself or herself a healer, expresses the ministry in that way where hysterical collapses may be numerous as people are 'slain by the Spirit'. Signs and wonders are promised if not guaranteed and so on. It is not my purpose here to decry those who engage in the healing ministry which is expressed in other ways, however anxious one can be over generalised claims of cures and miracles (a common failing in the wider healing field). God works in diverse ways for there are 'varieties of gifts'[28] and the Spirit, like the wind, 'blows where it wills'.[29] All of us must be careful about confining the Holy Spirit within *our* orthodoxy, *our* ecclesiastical structures, *our* method. Equally, while taking our own positive stance on the only premise we know, namely that it is the risen Christ who is the healer and that healing is through him, we do not spend our time and energy condemning good work coming from people who do not share our point of view.

Jesus appeared a little more flexible round the edges in an incident in which the disciples seemed to demand condemnation of someone involved in a ministry of healing who was 'not of us'.[30] In fact, he suggested, as he did to Peter (quoted above), that it was more important to get on with their own positive ministry than to use the energy and time condemning someone else.

There are approaches to healing about which we must warn. There are methods used—for example, at some of those dramatic, public occasions—which are not, in the long run, beneficial because they do not conduce to wholeness, although they may temporarily appear to cure. It is the anxiety about some of these other approaches that leads many to be cautious of involvement in the healing ministry and even to be highly critical of it. The essential and important point is that the recovery of the healing ministry as I am presenting it in this book is on a wider, but scriptural, basis. I shall, in my next chapter, define phrases like 'the ministry of healing' in such a way as to present the breadth of approach I seek to offer in terms of health and healing. When that breadth is explained[31] and understood, the attraction of this ministry and its nature, rooted in the Gospel, is usually appreciated and accepted.

The fact that there has been, across the denominations, an emerging interest in the healing ministry cannot be coincidence or even synchronicity. The Christian will see this process as one in which the Spirit is at work.

The second significant development—very important for the whole area of health and healing—is the new openness in medicine to the view that there are factors other than physical factors which condition the way an illness develops or may even be the cause of an illness. I will consider the implications of this point of view in the next two chapters. It is sufficient to say here that this willingness to take account of the influences of psychosomatic factors in illness is very encouraging to a body like The Churches' Council which has maintained this view for a long time.

It is not a new point of view, of course, for many doctors do look and have looked at illness in this way, but generally the scientific, materialistic background which is an essential part of us all—especially if we are in the second half of life—makes it difficult to conceive that events other than physical bring about illness. There is, however, increasing evidence that doctors are also open to the influence of *spiritual* factors in illness too.

The word spiritual is a problem word, for it means different things to different people. This is equally true on the church side. I may feel it necessary to return to that question. There are varied definitions of the word spiritual. They vary between a humanistic, 'theology from below' view, which thinks of spiritual as the 'dynamic-creative energies' of a human being, and a 'theology from above' view[32] which sees Spiritual as a concept related to the 'divine activity' in life.

The use of the word spiritual (with a lower case 's') and Spiritual (with a capital S), is taken from Paul Tillich[33] who uses this typographical method of distinguishing the uses of this word. In relation to the point I am making, but only in that sense, it does not really matter. General Practitioners are used to seeing humanity in terms of physical, psychological and social aspects of being. The addition of spiritual would be an enormous change for them.

I recall an eminent doctor who had made this point in a letter to the journal of The Royal College of General Practitioners, expressing the view that he simply could not understand the word spiritual in any sense at all. (His willingness to try to do so was expressed in his presence at a major event— the opening of the St Marylebone Healing and Counselling Centre, of which I shall say more later—which was certainly held in a very spiritual place and context!) But many doctors *are* looking at health and illness in a wider way.

In its last issue of 1983, the *British Medical Journal* devoted six of its pages to spiritual healing. In 1984 I, Bishop Maddocks and three colleagues spent a morning with the British Medical Association's (BMA) special working party on (as they called it) 'Alternative Therapy'.[34] The British Holistic Medical Association has been set up and many distinguished doctors belong to it. It exists to make prominent the concept of holistic health, that is health seen in relation to the whole person, as part of a wider movement to that end.

The Royal College of General Practitioners has had a working party with The Churches' Council for Health and Healing (CCHH) for two years, and the theme under discussion—and it was selected by the doctors—is 'Whole Person Medicine'.

I see the change in the medical point of view as very significant. I believe it is right that we interpret it as another 'straw in the wind of the Spirit'. It is wholly biblical to believe, as events in the prophecies of Isaiah involving the pagan Cyrus remind us,[35] that God works through people who do not acknowledge him and through human situations in which only those with eyes to see will 'see' his presence. Few doctors will see themselves as part of the ministry of healing but, as I shall argue in the next chapter, the medical discipline *is* a gift of God. That there is such a change in medicine—at the same time as the church is recovering, in such a notable fashion, its own call to healing ministry—is indeed providential. 'The Spirit is here'—the marvellous implication is that the opportunity for clergy–doctor co-operation is greater now than it has been in living memory.

When Archbishop William Temple inaugurated CCHH over forty years ago, its prime function was to encourage dialogue between religion and medicine. A man before his time, and therefore truly a prophet, he would have rejoiced to see the current increase in closer medical–religious co-operation. Others have worked to that end too, notably The Institute of Religion and Medicine, also based at St Marylebone Healing and Counselling Centre. Such co-operation is no longer a mere dream. The door is open more widely to such co-operation, and hopefully especially at local level, just because of the greater area of shared view about the causes and conditioning factors in illness today.

It is indeed a day of opportunity. The time has come for real effort at local levels to incarnate ministry by doctor and priest and counsellor together to help people to be more whole.

I end this chapter with an anecdote, a cameo that gave me particular pleasure.

In 1986, as Director of CCHH, I initiated and produced a video called *The Healing Ministry*.[36] It sought to present, in visual terms with a commentary, the concept of the healing ministry which I will present in this book. The video was booked by a BMA division in central England and I was asked to go and speak to it.

The usual attendance at this regular meeting, I was told, was 12 to 15. To my horror (I use the word with forethought),

I found gathered in the cafeteria and then formally in the Lecture Hall of the School of Nursing, 120 people, 100 of whom were general practitioners, consultants, nurses, and so on. The 20—and this is the marvellous point—were clergy who had been invited to come *by the doctors*!

It has been a matter of common practice for us to encourage churches to invite members of the medical profession to conferences, study days and other events held under the banner of the healing ministry. But here, the whole situation had been transposed. Here we had doctors inviting clergy to come and look at a video on the Christian healing ministry!

The incident was a small one, but it said a great deal to me about the recovery of the healing ministry in our time.

Notes to Chapter 1

1   Morton Kelsey, *Healing and Christianity* (SCM Press, London, 1973)
2   Cameron Peddie, *The Forgotten Talent* (first published by Fontana, 1966. Now published in a new edition, by Arthur James, 1985.)
3   John 21:22, *New English Bible*
4   Acts 8:9–24
5   Acts 4:1–31
6   Acts 4:31
7   Isaiah 6:5
8   Exodus 3:5
9   I Timothy 1:15
10 II Corinthians 12:9
11 Hebrews 6:6, Authorised Version
12 Matthew 10:7–8
13 John 14:6
14 Matthew 11:28
15 Matthew 11:2–5. I will expand this point in chapter 4.
16 John 7:53, 8:11. The authority of this passage has been questioned, but it has, in J B Phillips' phrase, 'a ring of truth' about it. Denis Duncan, Editor, *Through the Year with J B Phillips* (Arthur James, 1983), pp 42–43
17 Luke 7:37–50
18 Morris Maddocks, *The Christian Healing Ministry* (SPCK, 1981)

19   Morris Maddocks, *Christian Adventure* (SPCK, 1983)
20   Morris Maddocks, *Journey to Wholeness* (SPCK, 1986)
21   Morris Maddocks, *A Healing House of Prayer* (Hodder & Stoughton, 1987)
22   Leslie Weatherhead, *A Private House of Prayer* (first published by Hodder & Stoughton, 1958. Now published in a new edition by Arthur James, 1985.)
23   *The Acorn Healing Trust*, Whitehill Chase, Bordon, Hampshire.
24   The United Reformed Church, 86 Tavistock Place, London WC1; membership (in 1985, as per *UK Christian Handbook*) 135 000.
25   Available from the United Reformed Church, see note 24 above.
26   The Churches' Council for Health and Healing, St Marylebone Healing and Counselling Centre, Marylebone Road, London NW1 5LT. It is colloquially referred to as CCHH.
27   For example, The Guild of Health, The Guild of St Raphael, The Divine Healing Mission and many others including the Homes and Centres of Healing listed in 'Residential and Day Centres of Christian Healing', available from CCHH, see note 26 above.
28   I Corinthians 12:4
29   John 3:8
30   Mark 9:38–40
31   It has been a major part of my recent ministry as Director of CCHH to present a balanced view of healing ministry.
32   The phrases 'theology from below' and 'theology from above' come from David Schweizer who sees all theological positions classified within these terms.
33   Paul Tillich, *Systematic Theology* (SCM Press, London, 1978) the section on The Divine Presence.
34   The report of the Board of Science Working Party of the British Medical Association on *Alternative Therapy* (1986).
35   Isaiah 44:28, 45:1
36   *The Healing Ministry*, runs for approximately 46 minutes, with a slightly shorter edition of 37 minutes, now available for sale or hire, in VHS and Betamax, from CCHH, see note 26 above.

2

The Healing Spectrum

Phrases like 'the ministry of healing' or 'healing ministry' have become part of the language and literature of today. In this chapter I want to define 'healing ministry' in terms of my approach to the whole question of health and healing.

I use such phrases in two ways, first in a limited or narrower sense, but also in a much wider way that is summed up in my chapter heading, 'The Healing Spectrum'.

First, let me deal with the narrower and more limited way though, of course, the limitations refer only to classification in that I am confining the phrase to a particular sphere or discipline, in this case the religious sphere. It is not related at all to any limitation in power or productivity.

'The ministry of healing' is used to describe the particular contribution which the Christian Church makes to help people to be more whole. It comes from a context in which there are convictions about God, Jesus, the Holy Spirit, the healing community, faith, prayer, and so on. It believes that it is God's wish and will that we should be whole. This is, of course, a concept with an eschatalogical element to it. By that I mean that wholeness can only be complete beyond this life. Our ultimate wholeness belongs to the life after death.

The church believes that through the grace which is in Christ Jesus an element in our wholeness—which Christians see as crucial—is provided. 'Thanks be to God' cries St Paul, seeing himself delivered from 'this body of death'.[1]

The church believes that there is a *dunamis*, a dynamo, a power given by the Holy Spirit of whom, significantly, the word *energeia* is used in the New Testament. The power to be witnesses to Jesus was promised to the apostles when Jesus ascended into heaven[2] and was received at Pentecost.[3] Turning to another version of the giving of the Holy Spirit, it was given through Jesus breathing on the disciples, after his resurrection.[4]

The reality of the gift of the Spirit has never been doubted by the Church. It is, as Paul Tillich said,[5] the 'Divine activity' at work, in man and in the world. Where the Spirit is present, ordinary men and women are transformed and become capable of service, ministry and gifts quite beyond their expectation or understanding.[6] 'Gifts of healings'[7] are specifically included in the list of diverse gifts provided by St Paul. The gifts of preaching and healing were made possible when the apostles, as I mentioned above, were all filled with the Holy Spirit.[8]

Because of the specific demand made by Jesus of his disciples who were later to become, in the process of organisation and formalisation, 'the church', that they were to be his witnesses[9] and proclaim the Gospel to the uttermost part of the earth,[10] the church is committed to a preaching –healing ministry. It is therefore incumbent upon it to be a preaching community and at the same time a healing community.

The implications of that concept will be dealt with later in chapter 6. The point to be made here is that 'the ministry of healing', for the church, is the offer to human beings of wholeness and it is that which, by its nature, convictions and promised power, the church alone, representing Jesus, can give.

The ministry of healing in this narrower but essential sense is therefore expressed in ways appropriate to and springing from the church's theology, beliefs and mission. These will not necessarily be confined to, but will certainly include, prayer and intercession, blessing by the laying on of hands, anointing (in many traditions and certainly a practice based on the Bible in the famous passage in James' epistle),[11] healing relationship,[12] 'the healing of the memories',[13] counselling, spiritual direction, and so on. This is certainly a list of items that can properly be called 'means of grace'.[14] The church's healing ministry is an expression of the redemptive acts of God in Jesus Christ and the means of grace are those God–given ways by which we are helped to grow in grace and in the likeness of Jesus until we become whole.

It is the testimony of the Christian Gospel that without that element of redemption and grace we cannot be whole. This, I repeat, is no arrogant statement that excludes non–Christians from salvation and wholeness but simply a statement of the understanding of the Christian from within his standpoint in the faith that justification (or the restoration of our right relationship with God through Christ[15]) and sanctification (that is growth in grace towards wholeness), are accomplished through Christ. In the Christian view only the grace of Christ is able to deal with the fundamental dilemma of human nature, human sin and the hope of salvation. Excellent and worthy disciplines such as education, scientific knowledge, philosophy and psychology, each of which has contributed enormously as the gifts of God which they are in relation to human well-being, cannot meet the ultimate human needs. The essential human dilemma is a spiritual one which knowledge, training, self-understanding or scientific control through extended skills, insight and achievement cannot reach. It is 'the grace which is in Christ Jesus' that can reach down to, and deal with, that human dilemma.

It is not evolutionary progress in any human discipline that leads to life (it may help aspects of living)—it is the gift of God in redemption.

It is not the function of this book to look at theological and philosophical questions about how those who take stances other than that adopted here, that is within the Christian faith, may be saved, neither is it my obligation to lay down that God has no way of bringing those who stand outside the Christian faith to wholeness. That would constitute an arrogance which limits God's activity to *our* way. I write here from *within* the Christian standpoint and I cannot, from there, see the way to salvation apart from acceptance in faith of the grace-full and saving acts of the Christian's God. Healing ministry must therefore, for me and for the Christian church, be Christ-centred. It is the risen Christ who is the Healer.

It is this fundamental conviction that sees the Christian healing ministry—or the ministry of healing—as the essential element in the healing spectrum. And it is this redemptive element which is expressed in the means of grace (as I have described them) listed above. I hope to deal later with practical aspects of particular processes represented by some of these 'means of grace'.

Second, 'the ministry of healing' is a phrase that can be and is used in a much wider way. I have mentioned one key specific element in the healing spectrum—the Christian contribution, the gift of redemption. I turn now to the gifts of God, given for our wholeness. These are the gifts of creation.[16] God has provided many things that, rightly used, minister to our wholeness by helping us in one or another area of our being, mental, emotional and physical.

Primary is all that is offered to us through medicine. The medical discipline is the *first* of God's gifts for our healing.

This statement has several immediate practical implications.

First of all, it underlines that, *always*, those to whom we minister in the healing ministry must be encouraged to be in contact with their medical practitioner. I say this obviously in the desirable sense for, if healing services are to be part of the church's healing ministry, it is simply not possible to ensure that everyone to whom we minister *is* in touch with their doctor. What I am laying down is a principle. It is that healing ministry, as I emphasised above, is offered *in co-operation with medicine and not in place of it.*

This leads to the second principle which is that, in healing ministry, we do not and must not talk of the church's healing ministry—and this the British Medical Association did in the report already referred to[17] —as an alternative therapy. The word *alternative* is wholly inappropriate in the field of healing ministry and should not be used at all. It is the word *complementary* that is appropriate for at all times doctor and priest—and others—are working together, providing the different aspects of healing represented by their disciplines to make people more whole.

The whole case—and a proper case it is—for clergy-doctor co-operation is based on the understanding that their ministries/services are complementary, and in no way contradictory to each other. They are not alternative 'treatments'. The thrust in contemporary healing ministry is to strengthen the bond between the doctor and the priest/minister in the interests of the patient/person.

This is not in any way a defence of all that medicine does. Whatever gifts of knowledge and insight God gives can be abused and there are many who feel there is much in medical practice to be so criticised. That this is so is not in doubt—there is drug abuse as well as drug benefit. But the criticism is not one to be confined only to the medical discipline. Where there is human freedom—and indeed because there is human sin and the corruption that follows it—God's gifts are always open to abuse. The growth of the ecology party and the strong pressures from conservationists are responses to other abuses of knowledge in the scientific and technological area and are proper and necessary protests against the desecration of the world of nature. There is a constant need for watchfulness in relation to medical practice and policy. That is one reason for the need to study ethical problems in medicine today. Indeed the problems are arising from the ability to create life as much as—as it used to be—to destroy it.

These questions lie outside the scope of this book and certainly the ability of its author. The recording of them is intended to establish the point that the wrong use or abuse of God's gifts does not change the fact that they are his gifts. The sophisticated development of medicine and surgery is testimony to man's skill, but there could be no such development at all had creation not contained the material on which human beings can work.

There is a major testimony to the place of the doctor in the Apocryphal book, Ecclesiasticus.

Honour the doctor for his services,
for the Lord created him.
His skill comes from the Most High,
and he is rewarded by kings.
The doctor's knowledge gives him high standing
and wins him the admiration of the great.
The Lord has created medicines from the earth,
and a sensible man will not disparage them.
Was it not a tree that sweetened water
and so disclosed its properties?
The Lord has imparted knowledge to men,
that by their use of his marvels he may win praise;
by using them the doctor relieves pain

and from them the pharmacist makes up his mixture.
There is no end to the works of the Lord,
who spreads health over the whole world.

My son if you have an illness, do not neglect it,
but pray to the Lord, and he will heal you.
Renounce your faults, amend your ways,
and cleanse your heart from all sin.
Bring a savoury offering and bring flour for a token
and pour oil on the sacrifice; be as generous as you can.
Then call in the doctor, for the Lord created him;
do not let him leave you, for you need him.
There may come a time when your recovery is in their hands;
then they too will pray to the Lord
to give them success in relieving pain
and finding a cure to save their patient's life.
When a man has sinned against his Maker,
let him put himself in the doctor's hands.

Ecclesiasticus 38:1–15

The literalist who seeks to try to prove that medicine is not God's gift will not accept this as scriptural confirmation of the basic point that I am making. The Apocrypha is not regarded as that kind of authority by some Christians. (I say this because a doctor I met recently claimed that medicine was in fact 'of the devil'. She referred to many unsatisfactory practices taking place within medicine, of which she claimed personal knowledge, as the reason for withdrawing from it.) The point is not however dependent on finding a text to say that God gave humanity such gifts to help him/her to be restored to physical health, but on our understanding of God's good creation and providential love.

A *second* gift from God for our healing, especially if our dis – ease is in the mental or emotional area of our being, is contained in the knowledge and skills that are expressed in the counselling, psychotherapeutic and psychiatric disciplines. I shall say something about the nature and purpose of counselling later when I discuss aspects of 'healing relationship'. Here I simply want to draw attention to treatments or ministries (depending on how the practitioner looks at it) given in God's providence to enable wholeness to be restored in inner areas of disquiet and disturbance. It is also worth remembering that counselling and psychotherapy are not only curative or therapeutic processes but are growth processes too. While counsellors and therapists generally spend most of their time—and some even spend all of it—in the former sort of work, it is indeed proper to remember that normal, healthy people who nevertheless want to grow, mature and develop their inner resources and creative gifts, may well find a healing relationship of this kind highly productive.

A *third* element in the healing spectrum is music. This may be a novel thought to some but the proposition, if thoughtfully considered, will be seen to be a valid therapeutic discipline. This, of course, is not the sole or whole function of music, but it certainly can be a way in which music can give an added blessing.

Music ministry—or therapy—is one of the components in the dramatic new expression of 'whole person ministry' in the St Marylebone Healing and Counselling Centre in London. (This was opened by The Prince of Wales in July 1987 and dedicated some months later.)

The 'Vision of St Marylebone', as it has been called in *Health is for God*[18] is that which 'came' to the Rector of St Marylebone, Christopher Hamel Cooke, author of that book. Having come to the famous St Marylebone Parish Church, (in Marylebone Road, London, almost opposite Madame Tussauds), to make it, among others things, a base for the development of a wider healing ministry from which he could go out to lecture, speak, and so on, Christopher Hamel Cooke found a completely new opportunity to express that ministry, not outside his church, but underneath it. There, a very extensive Crypt had been used as a burial place. The Crypt was cleared of the huge number of coffins which occupied its vaults and proper and seemly re-burial took place in a cemetery in Surrey. Christopher Hamel Cooke is wont to say, when talking of the Crypt, that he saw it as a place that could be used for the living rather than by the dead. The way in which it could be used was as a centre for healing and counselling which would express the 'holistic' vision in a Christian context. So the £1 500 000 reconstruction was set in motion and the Crypt is now operating as such a centre.

This is not the place to embark on a full description of this great 'Vision of St Marylebone'. Details about it can be had from the Centre itself.[19] What is important is its bringing together of different disciplines committed to expressing a desire and determination to help people to be more whole.

There are four groups involved in this as it is intended to be, and must become, corporate ministry to wholeness. *First*, there is the church's healing and counselling ministry. This is expressed by the Pastoral Centre, itself operated by St Marylebone Parish Church. A team of Befrienders and Counsellors is available all day, every day[20] to offer help to those who drop in with varying needs or come by appointment to see the Chaplain or one of the team.

Second, there is the medical practice in which Dr Patrick Pietroni, widely known for his interest in the holistic approach to medicine (he was one of the founders of the British Holistic Medical Association in 1985), and his team of doctors, nurses, administrator, counsellor, secretaries and researchers work. The practice functions as a normal surgery (by National Health Service rules it had to be a local practice that would move into the Crypt),[21] but offers some complementary approaches not available in all practices. It also has a research team studying the effects of the holistic approach taken by the practice.

Third, there are 'the healing agencies' which have their offices in the Crypt. The Churches' Council for Health and Healing, being the national co-ordinating body it is,[22] has the largest suite of offices. The other groups are the Institute of Religion and Medicine, the Guild of St Raphael and the Order of St Luke.

Fourth—and it was for this reason that I introduced the St Marylebone Centre for Healing and Counselling into this section—there is the Music Therapy Unit where a team of music therapists who are Christians, help those who are disturbed, to find a way towards a greater wholeness. This approach to healing has had impressive results with children and is showing itself to be a way of offering therapy that brings results not able to be produced through other approaches.

It is worth recording that St Marylebone is the Parish

Church of Harley Street and is therefore appropriately forging real working links between religion and medicine. The Royal Academy of Music is also in the parish and is making significant links with healing through music.

A *fourth* element in the healing spectrum is what I have already called healing relationship. I want to give it its own chapter in order to make an important point—namely that God uses people to help other people to be whole. This is manifestly true whether you look at Ananias who was called on by God to help Paul through to his new beginning[23] or at the primary decision Jesus made in choosing 12 disciples who would preach the Kingdom, heal the sick and cast out demons. Every Christian, by virtue of his or her membership of the church, the healing community, is called to be part of the healing spectrum, God's gifts for our wholeness.

And *fifth*, there is the area of complementary medicine. This is a controversial area because it takes in a very wide field in which the valid is found beside the bizarre, the reasonably structured and organised therapy with proper training is found beside the totally *ad hoc* agency, where training takes only a weekend and trainers have no recognisable qualifications. I shall make a further comment on this at a later stage in the book. What is clear and is important here is that within the complementary field there are healing methods which are positive, creative, informed and responsible. In that area we shall therefore find further new knowledge (or indeed rediscover old and traditional knowledge) that represents yet more of that wide range of gifts given by God for our wholeness.

The healing ministry, using the phrase in this wider way, is a whole spectrum of gifts with, as an essential part of it, God's gift of redemption expressed in the church's healing ministry. In situations of illness which will include disease within, the healing ministries that we need are any of those several disciplines taken from the healing spectrum which are appropriate to specific needs. This will always include the doctor whom anyone who is ill should be seeing, but it may be that some other ministry is needed too. Perhaps there is an area of great immaturity in the emotional life that needs the psychotherapist. Perhaps there is some disquiet within a person that a healing relationship—whether with a friend, pastoral carer or pastoral counsellor—can help relieve. The church's ministry with its assurance of forgiveness and new beginning will deal best with guilt or failure to forgive.

Very often, ministry by laying on of hands will provide blessing and the upbuilding of the spiritual resources that are needed to deal with situations causing distress of mind and possibly disease of body. (Psychosomatic symptoms may well be indicating inner turmoils).

Laying on of hands[24] is not some kind of magic, administered by the church and immediately producing deliverance from every bodily or mental problem. It is, in the liturgical context, a declaration of God's desire that men and women be made whole, and a symbolic action through which grace and power may come. It is a potent symbol, a purposeful sign and a true seal implying the presence, peace and power of the risen Lord. It is in truth a means of grace. But it may not, nevertheless, always be the first step to be taken. Sometimes we have to prepare the way of the Lord. In this context a counselling ministry may need to precede the laying on of hands. The importance and value of the enabling ministry of preparation should never be underrated. It is not within our power to produce miracles. It may be our function to play a part in setting up situations in which a miracle can happen. The agent of that miracle is the Lord. It is a privilege indeed to be called to prepare the way for him to show the signs and wonders.

The healing spectrum implies a need for varied ministries. The variety of need comes from our being human and having aspects of that being which are physical, mental, emotional and spiritual. It is the variety of our need which makes it essential that a true holism be the basis of all that we seek to do when, in Jesus' name, we try to help people to become more whole.

Notes to Chapter 2

1   Romans 7:24
2   Acts 1:8

3   Acts 2:1–7
4   John 20:22
5   Paul Tilloch, *Systematic Theology*
6   Acts 4:13 and many other places.
7   I Corinthians 12:9
8   Acts 4:31
9   Acts 1:8
10 *Ibid*
11 James 5:14
12 This theme will be explored in chapter 6.
13 This theme will be discussed in chapter 10.
14 This may be an extension of the phrase as traditionally used, but the intention is clear.
15 William Barclay always speaks in terms of restored relationship with God as his understanding of words like justification.
16 Christopher Hamel Cooke, more than others, has dealt with the theme of creation in relation to the healing ministry. See his book *Health is for God* (Arthur James 1986).
17 The Report of the Board of Science Working Party of the British Medical Association on *Alternative Therapy* (1986).
18 Christopher Hamel Cooke, *Health is for God* (Arthur James, 1986)
19 The Centre's address is: St Marylebone Healing and Counselling Centre, St Marylebone Parish Church, Marylebone Road, London NW1 5LT.
20 Times should be checked as they will change with development.
21 The local practice from where the new surgery was set up was in Lisson Grove Health Centre in London NW1.
22 For information about CCHH, write to: CCHH, St Marylebone Parish Church, Marylebone Road, London NW1 5LT.
23 Acts 9:10–22. See chapter 9 for a fuller discussion of this event.
24 Notes on laying on of hands are included in chapter 12.

3

Whole Person Healing

At the heart of everything that is said, or to be said, about the ministry of healing, is the proposition that human beings are not simply bodies but have minds, hearts and souls. In other words, there are mental, emotional and spiritual aspects to our being, in addition to the physical. This is confirmed by the form of the so-called 'golden rule': 'Love the Lord your God with all your heart, with all your soul, with all your strength, and with all your mind'.[1]

Before discussing whole person healing—or a holistic and indeed, as I shall argue, truly holy approach to health—it is important to stress that it is only for the purposes of theoretical analysis and discussion that we analyse ourselves in this way. The purpose is however a highly practical one. I deliberately avoid the use of the word 'parts'—a physical part, a spiritual part, and so on—for such a process mitigates against my plea to us all to see man and woman in their wholeness. Man *is* a living soul, rather than *has* a soul. The Bible testifies to that concept of unity. The Hebrew word *shalom* especially expresses the totality of our relationship—to God 'upwards', to the earth 'downwards', to others 'outwards' and to ourselves 'inwards'. *Shalom* or peace is the gift we want because it is a blessing on us in relationship. It is within all these relationships that we live and move and have our being. It is however proper to think of aspects (which is the word I choose) of our being and it is necessary to do so in order to make fundamental points about health, illness and the ministry of healing.

The essential principle that I am establishing here is that there are factors in illness other than purely physical factors. Such factors may play a part in the development of an illness and possibly in causing it.

37

This principle is not new. It has always been present, at least by implication, in the religious view of life although it has not been consciously acted on in ways which are stressed today. It is not new in psychology, for the psychotherapeutic/ analytic approach has seen the importance of illness both in terms of its nature and its timing, as diagnostic clues to disease and therefore as a means to therapeutic advancement. What is the more novel feature of the present situation is the willingness of many in the medical profession to see psychosomatic factors not as interesting additional information, but as of the essence of the problem. 'What does this mean?', the primary medical question in the evaluation of symptoms, is now carried over to the much greater question, fundamental in a holistic approach, 'What does this mean in relation to the whole person affected by it?'. It is the importance given to such psychosomatic factors that has moved much more to the centre of the stage in our time. The insights coming to the church from the recovery of the healing ministry and the new openness in medicine open the door to medical-religious co-operation both at national and at local levels.[2]

Orthodox medicine has traditionally taught, and still teaches, that man is a physical, psychological and social being. Within that tripartite description there is a recognition of non-physical factors that contribute to illness. By implication, there is a similar recognition of these factors in healing/ curing. But while the theory has been clear, the extraordinary progress to sophistication in 'physical' treatment (that is, in orthodox medicine) has tended to make it dominant in surgeries and hospitals.

There are, of course, exceptions to this generalisation. I write of the dominant trends. The pressure towards emphasis on 'the physical' has, of course, been encouraged by the scientific-materialistic ethos by which we all—certainly the over-40s—have been conditioned. And in saying this I am thinking not only of the medical profession. One of the reasons for the deficiency in spirituality seen in many churches—and in perhaps each one of us—is our inability to see, or certainly *feel*, with Paul that 'the things that are seen are transient, but the things that are unseen are eternal'.[3]

Because of our conditioning by the scientific emphases of our society and our times, it is much easier to believe that what we see, touch and handle is the real.

It follows from this that the 'eternal' or spiritual dimension has been seen and is seen as unreality and that involvement in it belongs to the ethereal rather than to reality. It is therefore essentially an escape from the real world. Nothing is further from the truth. It is of crucial importance to understand that the more we involve ourselves in the eternal, the spiritual, the more we are compelled to be involved in the temporal in proclamation and compassion.[4] Of this the Incarnation was the supreme example. It was precisely because Jesus was 'one with the Father'[5] that he shared our life and its pain to the point where he had to endure the reality of crucifixion for the sake of us all. The Christian stance on reality is therefore St Paul's statement quoted above—a statement which 'stands on its head' our understanding of what is real. And if the Christian perspective is based on that Pauline view of the spiritual as reality, everything the church says and does is coming out of a theology, which is contrary to the world's view of life and being.

That theology includes a 'doctrine of man' who is made in the image of God, who in disobedience has damaged his relationship with God and who, through Christ, is restored to a right relationship with God.[6] The Christian view of man is one that cannot do anything other than include that divine-human relationship and that relationship is spiritual. It is therefore not just harmony we seek, but a holy harmony.

It is this spiritual dimension that is not included in the medical definition expressed in their tripartite view (physical, psychological, social). It is for the specific addition of the spiritual dimension that the church pleads in the understanding of human 'being'.

It is sometimes helpful to visualise a concept which has to be expressed theoretically. In figure (i) I have set down something of my understanding of the relationship between the physical, emotional, mental and spiritual aspects of our make-up.

I stress again that it is only for exploratory reasons that we analyse 'being' in this way. I also stress that no symbol should

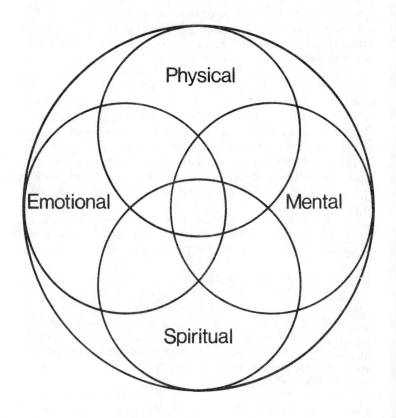

Figure 1: *The relationship between aspects of our make-up*

be pushed beyond its limits. Indeed it may be helpful for readers to try to express for themselves, in a symbolic way, their understanding of this four-fold relationship between the physical, emotional, mental and spiritual parts of our being.

There are a number of important statements expressed in this symbol which, I hope, is one that those committed to a spiritual interpretation of life, whether Christian or non-Christian, could accept in principle. There are Christian language phrases in my description of the symbol, but they do not affect the basic points I am making:[7]

1 The symbol is essentially one large circle and a circle is traditionally a symbol of wholeness.

2 The four small circles represent the four aspects with which we are dealing. I have shown them as taken into our being.

a) *Physical*: God has given us bodies which are to be used to his glory. It is therefore our responsibility to develop them, not to some theoretical physical perfection, but to the best that they can be. There is a fundamental inequality in life in that we all have bodies with different potential, based on inherited biological factors, and so it is not possible for us all to become 'Atlas-type' men or 'Venus-type' women in the form of physical perfection. We can only become the best possible. But to aim at that is our obligation to God.

This leads obviously into a whole area of important considerations on which I cannot expand in this volume but which are essentially summed up in the words *discipline* and *self-discipline*. They include physical fitness, diet, smoking, alcohol drinking, leisure, rest, and so on. Our attitudes to such physical matters will depend on our perceived personal responsibility for our bodies as 'the temple of the Holy Spirit'.[8] Here my purpose is simply to underline our obligation to deal with our physical bodies so that they develop into that best and are therefore of use in our service to God.

b) *Mental*: The same principle applies to the development of our minds. If we are going to give of our best in service to God and humanity, then the development of the full potential of our mental ability is an obligation on us.

It is also an obligation laid on society to ensure that the education system should enable that development, if education is understood in its full and proper meaning of 'leading out'[9] our potential and offering proper opportunity for the expression of all our creative abilities. This again clearly leads into another area I cannot go into in detail here—the whole philosophy and practice of education. Insofar as it is our responsibility to use every opportunity we can to stretch our minds, extend our knowledge and develop our creative gifts, we again have the obligation to do that and should see this as a duty to God who has created us with these abilities.

Fortunately, in this area of our being, we have greater flexibility in that while the body begins to deteriorate very quickly—for deterioration and ultimately death are, paradoxically, part of life—mental development is possible long into the years of life. The presence of senior citizens taking part in courses, Open University programmes, adult evening classes, and so on, is a happy manifestation of this fact.

c) *Emotional*: Just as there is physical growth and mental development, we should also grow emotionally towards maturity. If we do not so develop, we will have problems. The various theories of child development and the development of personality set out the 'normal' stages of growth.[10] If, because of factors in our early years, for example if a lack of love and consequent insecurity have been our experience, then we may not pass creatively through these stages. We may find ourselves stuck at some stage. That will, of course, prevent our forming good relationships at all.

It is the experience of those who have to deal with mid-life crises that over and over again there is a direct connection between unhappy experiences in very early years and later problems. Growth towards maturity has been blocked and emotional stresses, strains, anxieties and even more specific expressions of such disease occur.

Here again, the well-developed personality which has dealt constructively with difficulties along the way and has emerged into adult maturity is the hoped-for product in emotional terms. Immature people can be problem people. If we are going to be well-equipped for service, we have to grow in the emotional area too, and be qualified to cope with life.

d) *Spiritual*: The same sort of growth is desirable in this area. To be of service, the spiritual side of our being must develop also. In other words—if somewhat humanly speaking—just as we need to learn to relate to others in a mature and positive way, so the spiritual dimension in our life needs to grow through a creative relationship with God. Generally speaking, this schema would be felt to be true by all those concerned with the spiritual dimension. What is important to notice in the symbolic representation is that the four circles representing the four developed areas of our personality *interact with each other*. This brings me to the next point.

3 The physical, mental, emotional and spiritual areas of our being are interdependent so that if there is disease in any one area—for example, our emotional life or our spiritual life—this may express itself in disease in the body. It is in this interdependence that there lies the possibility of psychosomatic factors which can influence the development of illness or, on the positive side if dealt with creatively, development in our healing.

I do believe that the reality of this point does not require extensive proof to contemporary readers. I will confine myself to one or two comments.

First, it is manifestly obvious that loss of temper, furious rage and outbursts, will express themselves physically in raised blood pressure, and all that follows from that will affect the heart and so on. Negative emotional reaction to a situation will produce changes in the body for the worse, and conversely positive reactions in terms of attitude will be for the better.

A friend told me of a friend (I stress the need to be wholly confidential, hence these general terms) who, having gone to her general practitioner feeling unwell, was sent for x-rays. These came back showing that she had tuberculosis. The symptoms of that illness then began to be actively expressed by coughing and so on. Three weeks later, an urgent message from her doctor brought the news that the x-ray plate had been confused and in fact she did not have tuberculosis at all. The symptoms vanished overnight.

The symptoms came as a result of anxiety, and disappeared when there were no grounds for anxiety.

A young lady lived in the east end of a large city and at night worked, to make extra money, in her local pub as a barmaid, an exercise she enjoyed for the friendships it brought her. She married and moved into a quite different social context in a stock-broker belt area in the city. She developed a rash which was not serious in health terms, but was a nuisance. The doctor she consulted diagnosed it as eczema and dispensed treatment accordingly, but it made no difference to the rash. A second doctor acted similarly but, in view of the presence of the symptom, suggested a specialist consultation. The specialist, having heard the medical story, showed his wisdom by asking not so much about the physical symptoms, but about her as a person, and about changes in her life. She told him of her former work and her present marriage, her happiness but social loneliness. His prescription was surprising and simple: 'Get a job as a barmaid in a local pub'. She did, and the rash did not recur. It was a psychosomatic expression of emotional disease.

There are New Testament miracles that seem to point towards Jesus' ministering with this sort of inter-relationship in mind. There is the story of the man let down through the roof so that Jesus could minister to him.[11] This is a miracle which demonstrates a physical healing—'Rise, take up your pallet and walk',[12] but it is also one in which he forgives sins. This action led to the customary criticism as to his right to do such things, as forgive sins, but this criticism, and the argument that ensued would never have arisen if he had not declared the man forgiven. The miracle involved a physical cure, but Jesus seemed to be saying additionally that there was more needed by this man than simply a 'cure'. The illness, he seems to be suggesting, had connections with some situation (we do not know what it was) that needed forgiveness and that this was a necessary element in his being made well, and even more so in his total health.

Another example is the story recorded in John's Gospel about the man who had been trying to get into the pool outside the temple for over 30 years.[13] That he was, as the *Authorised Version* describes it, an 'impotent' man seems to be borne out by what he had failed to achieve. Surely he could, if he had really wanted to do so, found someone to help him to be the first to get into the pool? (It may also be a critical commentary on the community to which he belonged that he was never enabled to get there.) It is not surprising that Jesus asks him the important question 'Wilt thou be made whole?'.[14] The full impact of that question is perhaps best brought out by other translations of it as 'Do you *really* want to be well?' It is, as it was meant to be, a penetrating question. It is worth a short digression to consider the implications.

The answer we would all want to give to that question, and indeed to hear from others, would be 'Of course I want to be well! Who wants to be ill?'. But, in reality, people can, in fact, want to be ill, and indeed to be ill rather than well.

Illness may be needed to control a household in one's interest, to prevent situations changing and so on. There are sons and daughters, particularly 'only' ones, who whenever they might have wanted to marry or to emigrate found themselves prevented by parental illness which absolutely forbade their leaving home. Such illness is not necessarily consciously brought about. It may have its genesis in the unconscious, but the result is the same.[15] The exodus is prevented! The family members so affected have been successfully manipulated into staying at home and illness has been the medium of that successful manipulation.

Or again there are those in life who sadly have little of that which attracts love. In their desperation to get attention they may well resort to illness to ensure that they will have attention and affection. And if such a method of successful manipulation works well, it will be used again and again. When such a pattern has developed, it would be hard to let illness go. It is needed to make life tolerable. Illness can become a crutch we dare not be without. In such cases, our resistance to healing would be real. Not even God could heal us.[16]

In all situations of pastoral care, counselling or spiritual direction, we need to be aware of this kind of resistance to therapeutic or healing progress. We constantly have to ask

'What does this mean?' for it may not be the illness that is the matter in need of attention but the reasons for having to hold on to the illness. It is along this line of therapeutic enquiry that progress towards healing may be engendered.

After this digression, I go back to the story itself and the psychosomatic indications in it.

Jesus meets the man in the precincts of the temple and a conversation ensues. The final statement Jesus makes is a strong one. He says in effect: 'Yes, I have cured you of your illness' but 'go and sin no more, lest a worse thing come upon you'. In other words, the avoidance of a relapse in his case may well be related to inner change or a change in lifestyle. 'If you do not alter your way of living and behaving, you will be more ill than you were before.'

Whole person healing is the approach that must be developed if all the elements that make for illness are to be treated. While the doctor is an essential presence always—it is *never* part of healing ministry to exclude the doctor—it is also essential to have a place for ministry/treatment from those knowledgeable in matters of mental, emotional and spiritual concern.[17] We therefore draw from our healing spectrum whatever resources are appropriate to need. It may be that doctor and priest have to work together, or counsellor and minister, or music therapist and doctor and so on. It may be that laying on of hands is appropriate but there may be times when a considerable amount of preparation, perhaps through counselling, is necessary before such a service. Ministry by laying on of hands is not an exercise in magic! It does involve the person.[18]

The glory of the whole person approach to healing is that it recognises the many and diverse gifts of God for our healing and it encourages co-operation between the disciplines in the interests of each individual. I have no doubt that the next decade will show a tremendous increase in this aproach to treatment/ministry. That is why the further understanding of the healing ministry is one of the most exciting features of our times.

Is it however 'cure' or 'wholeness' that is central to this ministry? We must look at this question in the next chapter.

Notes to Chapter 3

1   Luke 10:27, *New English Bible*
2   A major emphasis in the report of the joint working party involving The Royal College of General Practitioners and The Churches' Council for Health and Healing (expected in 1988) is on medical-religious co-operation at local levels. The Institute of Religion and Medicine has as its main purpose such co-operation.
3   II Corinthians 4:18
4   The Iona Community has always incarnated this point. Clergy members of the Community will almost always be found ministering in industrial and other complex situations. Retreat was always with a view to greater involvement in the life of the world.
5   See the tenor of St John 17:21–22.
6   William Barclay constantly uses the phrase—about restoration to a right relationship with God—in his translation of the New Testament.
7   I shall say more of this specifically Christian factor later.
8   I Corinthians 6:19
9   From the Latin, *e-ducare*, which means to lead out.
10 See such writers as Erikson, Winnicott.
11 Mark 2:1–12
12 Mark 2:9
13 John 5:1–16, *Authorised Version*
14 John 5:6, *Authorised Version*
15 We shall discuss the unconscious in chapter 9.
16 The theme of divine-human co-operation is discussed in chapter 12.
17 Ecclesiasticus chapter 39, *New English Bible with Apocrypha*, is a marvellous statement about medicine and pharmacy as God-given gifts. Because it is in the Apocrypha, some may not regard it as having biblical authority, but it has, again recalling J B Phillips' phrase, 'a ring of truth' about it.
18 See note 16 above.

4

A Ministry to Wholeness

The focus in the Christian healing ministry is on wholeness rather than cure. This is an important statement for it draws the ministry away from those public dramatic forms with which, as I have already explained, it is often connected—to its detriment in the eyes of many; practices which bring anxiety, suspicion and mistrust—not least to clergy. God wants us, we believe, to be whole. That is the reason for the Incarnation of Jesus, his crucifixion, resurrection and the sanctifying presence of the Holy Spirit. It is something far greater than simply physical well-being that he seeks for us. In terms of the definition of human 'being' which we have established in our 'whole person' concept, that wholeness relates to the health we need in all the inter-related aspects of our being.

In the illustration I offered in the last chapter, the circles representing physical, mental, emotional and spiritual inter-relate in such a way that there is a space in the centre which is common to each interacting circle. This is I believe, what is called, in other ways of looking at human personality, our 'centre'. It is, as it were, the heart of our being. If we are as well as we can be at our centre, we have reason to be thankful—we are healthy indeed.

Another way in which I like to think of this central area is as our 'point of balance'. The concept of balance is an important one and we shall look at it more closely in the chapter on health.[1] That point of balance is, however, unique to each one of us for we are all different people. It is constituted by the way the aspects of *our* personality inter-relate. If the inter-relationship is good, we will again function as healthy people—we are balanced people.

It is not possible, however, to think of that centre as exactly the same for everyone. There are some whose possibility of physical development is limited from the beginning but, just because of that, there may be a compensatory element in their mental or their emotional or their spiritual area. Helen Keller had severe physical limitations, but she had enormous resources in other areas. She was a balanced, healthy and whole person in the true sense with a point of balance different from the physically well-developed person who had no such problems but who, not having such problems, had not developed the compensatory or balancing strengths which she had. We function best when we are in balance. When we have found our centre, we are on the way to wholeness.

The symbol I have created (and those interested in Jungian thought will note that it has worked out as a mandala-type symbol[2]), is, as I said earlier, one that would be acceptable to those who believe in a spiritual dimension but do not necessarily interpret that fact in Christian terms. Christianity must not arrogantly claim as its own the whole area of spirituality. It offers a particular form of spirituality, but not the only example of it. There must therefore be for the Christian a further element in the symbol that represents the presence and power of the Holy Spirit in enabling someone to move towards wholeness.

This takes us into a difficult area and one that cannot be fully examined within the limitations of this book. However it may be helpful to look a little more closely at the words *spirit* and *spiritual* as Tillich sees it—I have referred already to the typographical distinction he uses.[3] In a huge volume offering his theological system, he has a long section on The Divine Presence. At the very beginning of it he states his usage of the words spirit and spiritual. He says, as I noted earlier, that when he uses spirit with a small (that is a lower case) 's' he defines this as relating to 'the dynamic creative energies' in a human being. When he uses the same word with a capital 'S', he is referring to 'the Divine activity of the Holy Spirit'.

This distinction points to two concepts of spiritual which I have found to be operative in the healing and particularly counselling world. To be involved in a caring and/or loving relationship is to be spiritually engaged. Counselling, it is claimed, is then a spiritual undertaking by its very nature.

There is really no such thing as *Christian* counselling. There are counsellors who, as Christians, *implicitly* (but not explicitly, except in certain circumstances) bring their faith into their work. Others feel that while disputing nothing in this statement—loving care *is* a spiritual engagement—it omits an element essential to the Christian contribution. That is the Divine activity—the Holy Spirit—not immanent in a rather vague way, but transcendent, present and acknowledged.

I am inclined to believe, though I can only state it here as an intuition and not offer the research and reasons necessary to give this intuition validity, that the mainstream counselling movement has tended to be involved in the 'small s' spiritual philosophy that is working in the area of the 'dynamic-creative' part of our being (and essentially represents, in Schweitzer's classification of the two basic theological approaches, 'theology from below') while the 'charismatic' emphasis ('theology from above' in Schweitzer's classification) *explicitly* and deliberately uses the language of the faith, the means of grace (like prayer and laying on of hands) and consciously involves the presence and person of the Holy Spirit in the healing/therapeutic process.

There may be a problem here over *immanence* and *transcendence*. The counselling model tends to over-emphasise the immanent element in relation to the Divine presence, correspondingly diminishing or sometimes excluding, the transcendent element, while the charismatic approach has tended to reverse the emphasis. While over-emphasising (in terms of balance) the transcendence of God, it has under-emphasised the immanence. A wide gap has therefore evolved between counselling and the charismatic renewal movement and they still live, except in some individuals, uncomfortably together.[4] As it is very much part of my own ministry to work to bring these two approaches to a greater understanding of each other,[5] convinced that, however ungrammatical the statement is, God is more to be found in 'both/and' than in 'either/or', I find the excessive intolerance so often demonstrated by Christians who arrogantly claim to be right and elevate their 'either' into the only divine truth there can be, to be out of touch with the true spirit of the faith. Indeed, they are unlike the Jesus (to refer back to an incident already mentioned) who did not respond to the disciples request for a rebuke to someone engaged in healing ministry but who 'is not of us'.[6] Rather he rebuked the disciples for their intolerance and counselled the need to attend to one's own ministry faithfully, positively, empathetically, rather than use up effort in unnecessary negative criticisms.

I do not for one moment recommend an acceptance of over-liberal views, nor any diminution of the Christian witness. Indeed, I would veer in the other direction. As one committed to a biblical theology, the limits of acceptability for myself are clearly laid down. We must proclaim the stance we take positively and do it 'with boldness'.[7] But the emphasis is on commitment to our own positive ministry rather than engaging in the less fruitful but time-consuming task of knocking points of view with which we are not in sympathy, in a spirit of dogmatic and self-righteous intolerance. There is much genuine evil in the world in both action and propaganda that we need to attack. To condemn other Christians who are doing good work in Jesus' name because we differ from them in theory is not an act of grace. It is a spiritually risky undertaking calling other people's good evil just because it does not fit our own particular dogma.

I believe the sources of the gap in the use of the word and concept of spiritual that has evolved in our time goes a long way back towards the post-Reformation era and subsequent developments in understanding of the spiritual dimension or element. I hope that by working together, the shared purpose of helping people to find salvation, health, wholeness, holiness, healing (for all these words have the same root) will lead to an integration of the elements in what remains a divided witness. Meantime I believe that the illustration I offered requires something more than is represented by the four aspects which humanists and others not committed to the Christian faith can wholly share. If I have to put it into symbolic form, there must either be the addition of an element from outside the human being (the transcendent element) making its impact (the divine activity) at the very centre of our lives (see figure ii) or the addition of a second and greater circle endeavouring to express the over-arching presence and the redemptive love of God within which alone our wholeness can be complete (figure iii). The symbol must include the presence and effect of grace on our wholeness as Christians understand it if it is going to express the fullness of the healing ministry.

I have stated my belief that the ministry of healing is focussed on wholeness and I shall shortly underline that point in a particular way. I must not however write as if physical cure was either wrong in itself or undesirable. This would totally deny the witness of the Gospel to the work of Jesus.

The miracle stories in the Gospels contain many instances of physical illnesses healed and health restored. The Gospel does not in fact make the distinction between cure and wholeness in the language it uses—all are miracles of healing.[8] Jesus did restore sight and hearing, remove leprosy, banish fevers and, of course, cast out demons. It is also clear, to repeat an important point, that he saw such acts as signs of the presence and power of the Kingdom in his person. When John the Baptist sent a message from prison, asking Jesus if he was in fact the Messiah, the Lord's answer came back crystal clear: 'Go, tell John,' he said, 'that the deaf hear, the blind see, the lame walk, the dead are raised'.[9] The miracles are the authentication of his Messianic rôle and proof that the Kingdom has come in power in him.

Physical healing is not then unimportant. It is absolutely right that we should be free to ask for the taking away of a particular illness or limitation, especially if the illness is of a negative, destructive kind. Jesus did seem to attack disease as if it were something to be destroyed by Messianic power. That element of attack 'in the name of Jesus'—there is undoubtedly power in the *name* of Jesus—should be part of the healing ministry today. If the command of Jesus to his disciples to 'preach the Gospel and heal the sick'[10] —a command they obviously understood[11] —is a command to the church, the healing community, today, then the church has no way of escape from involvement in the healing ministry. It should indeed be, as I have already stressed, the normal work of the church.

That ministry will include ministering to those who seek physical healing. As we are not miracle workers, we can only do everything that we can to ensure that there is not

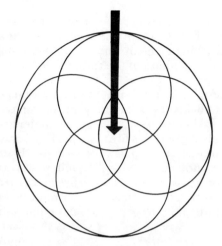

Figure 2: *The transcendent element making its impact*

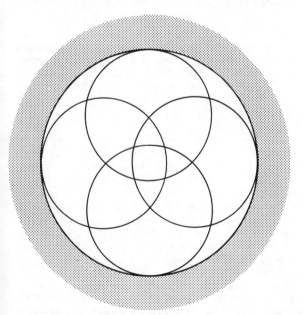

Figure 3: *The over-arching presence for our wholeness*

irresponsible expectation present. We place the prayer offered in the context of the Gethsemane attitude of 'Thy will be done'. With the teaching element very prominent in healing ministry always, a recognition of the right to seek physical cure remains.

That right clearly established, I return to the importance of seeing the healing ministry as 'a ministry to wholeness', a wholeness to be, as I said before, eschatalogically understood. It can be complete only beyond this life. The healing ministry proclaims and puts into action the gospel of salvation. Understood as a ministry to wholeness, the healing ministry is often expressed *not by the removal of suffering but through it*. This great theme I will take up in chapter 6. Meantime we must try, as I promised in the Introduction, to give some definition to the concept of health.

Notes to Chapter 4

1   See chapter 5.
2   'Mandala' is a Sanskrit word for a circle. 'The symbolism includes ... all concentrically arranged figures, round or square patterns with a centre, and radial or spherical arrangements'—Joseph Campbell, Editor, *The Portable Jung* (Penguin, 1976), note 4, paragraph 325.
3   See chapter 1, note 33.
4   This is my experience having spent many years in, as it were, both camps. As Associate Director and Training Supervisor at Westminster Pastoral Foundation, the national counselling and training centre in London founded by my friend and colleague the late Revd Bill Kyle, from 1972–1979, in my 17 years as Director of Highgate Counselling Centre in north London and in my rôle as Secretary and then Chairman of the World Association of Pastoral Care and Counselling, I was deeply involved with professional people—psychotherapists and analysts—who were trained in a way that made them very uncomfortable with evangelical, charismatic or 'healing' approaches. There was always anxiety over trainees with a 'Clinical Theology' background or training. I am speaking of the early and middle 70s when Frank Lake, the founder and director of the Clinical Theology Association, was a powerful presence and in some areas 'suspect' because of his personal evangelical stance.

In using the word 'evangelical', incidentally, I use it not to describe an extreme position. I am a minister of a church in the 'evangelical and reformed tradition', the Church of Scotland, and I am not prepared to give the word 'evangelical' away to particular emphases of a conservative kind.

Equally the mainstream counselling movement has been suspect to many in the more biblically based theological traditions. This was represented in the denominational balance in any 'year' of counselling trainees. The counselling background was seen to be too 'liberal', 'humanist', and so on, for those traditions. The tension between the two disciplines was, and is, real.

5   In my rôle at the time of writing this book—that is as Director of The Churches' Council for Health and Healing—I have to (try to) hold together a wide spectrum of theological positions. There are members of the Council from both the traditions and the approaches I have described in note 4 above, and I see it as part of my present purpose to do what I can to bring these diverse approaches close together. I believe the gap is narrowing. At least the area between the two is fuzzier than it was. In other words, there is less inflexibility and rigidity in this area. But the gap is indeed there.

6   Mark 9:38–40. This incident refers to someone healing in Jesus' name, so the situation is not wholly parallel to attitudes that may be felt to non-Christian healers. But the point I make remains valid. Jesus did not reflect the rigidity and exclusiveness the disciples seemed to expect.

7   Acts 4:13, 29, 31, where 'boldness' is mentioned three times.

8   The miracles include specifically 'physical' cures but, as I indicated above, in the two miracles I used to illustrate 'psychosomatic' factors in illness and healing, Jesus was concerned with wholeness too.

9   Matthew 11:2–6 and Luke 7:18–23 (paraphrased)

10   Matthew 10:7–8 (paraphrased)

11   Acts 4:29–30

5

The Definition of Health

The effort to formulate a satisfactory definition of health has occupied many minds and, in my experience, much committee and working party time! This implies clearly that there is a major difficulty in the project. It may be helpful to begin by recording some of the definitions of health that have been offered at various times in history.[1]

There is an inscription, written around the years 727–705BC which is attributed to the Assyrian ruler Sargon II. It embraces the essence of the quadrilateral that I have been using and which I have made the basis of my visual symbol. He prays to his gods to give him:

length of days
fitness of body
joy of heart
radiance of spirit

The earliest Greek word used for health is *isonomia* which means balance or equilibrium. I quote directly from the document, of which Dr John Wilkinson[2] was the author, which was helpful to the Standing Committee on Health and Healing of the General Assembly of the Church of Scotland[3]:

The earliest Greek word used for health in a technical sense was *isonomia*, which means balance or equilibrium. This referred to a proper balance of the four elements which were believed to make up the body, *viz* blood, phlegm, black bile and yellow bile. In classical Greek mythology, the positive and negative types of definition of health were symbolised in the myths of Hygieia, the goddess of health, and her father Aesculapius, the god of healing. The worshippers of Hygieia emphasised the positive concept of health as a natural state of

well-being to which men were entitled if they governed their
lives wisely. The myth of Aesculapius, on the other hand,
thought of health as the absence of disease, attained by treatment at the shrines of the god.

In the Old Testament, stress is laid on a right relationship
with God as the basis of health; in other words the 'righteousness' that grows out of faith in him and obedience to him and
his law. The product of righteousness is the *shalom* to which I
have already referred which means 'wholeness, serenity and
fulfilment'.[4]

The New Testament is essentially concerned with putting a
wrong situation right—that is the way in which our relationship with God, damaged by sin, is made good. Jesus came to
bring us back into a right relationship with God—and with
our brother and sister, ourselves and our world. The New
Testament therefore puts its emphasis on healing rather than
on health. The Good News is that there is a way back to a
right relationship with God. Jesus is the healer; Jesus offers
healing.

There is a Latin definition of health found in Juvenal, the
satirist. He recommends people to pray for a sound mind in a
sound body—*mens sana in corpore sano*.

In 1948 the World Health Organisation (WHO) produced
a definition of health which has, in some ways, become the
accepted definition. It runs:

Health is a state of complete physical, mental and social well-
being and not merely the absence of illness.

That puts health into a positive context (compare my earlier
point in counselling).[5]

We can, I think, all feel comfortable with that definition
although we may want to go further than it does. But it does
take in the physical, mental and social aspects and it does
underline the positive side of health.

Dr Wilkinson has, with his typical clarity of mind, set out a
number of propositions. I can do nothing more helpful than
quote these in full, with his permission:

1   *Health is a property of life.* Health belongs to a living organism. Only where there is life can there be wholeness, integration and harmony of being, function and relationship which is the essence of health. Health is also a quality of life which may vary: thus we speak of 'good health' and 'poor health'.

2   *Health is the gift of God.* As life itself is the gift of God, so is the health that goes with it. We cannot earn it or demand it but only accept it.

3   *Health is a means, not an end.* Health is not an end in itself, to be sought after for its own sake. It is the means by which he who possesses it may fulfil the end and the purpose of his life.

4   *Health is a responsibility.* Although health is originally a gift, its maintenance is a responsibility of man. It is not a state which automatically continues; it must be maintained, for it can be influenced for good or ill by the attitude and behaviour of its possessor.

5   *Health is a characteristic of the whole man.* The health of man is characterised by wholeness and harmony in his whole being, function and relationships. His health depends on his living in a right relationship to God and to himself, which in turn means that he is living in a right relationship to his fellows and to his environment.

6   *Health is a characteristic of body, mind and spirit.* The health of the body is characterised by its progressive growth and development to maturity, by its fitness and physical strength by which it is able to engage in physical activity, by its adaptability to changing conditions, and finally by a long life. The health of the body is demonstrated by an ability to resist disease, especially of an infectious nature, and by its power within certain limits to heal wounds and lesions inflicted upon its tissues.

The health of the mind is characterised by a continuing process of development and maturation which is accompanied by productive thought, creativity and happiness. Soundness of mind is demonstrated by an ability to cope with the normal events of life, and to face successfully its crises and conflicts.

Health of the spirit is characterised by spiritual growth in grace and the knowledge and experience of God, which results from an increasing faith in God, the worship of God, and the proper use of the means of grace which he has provided.

Clearly the ingredients of a satisfactory definition of health are in this sequence of propositions. Dr Wilkinson sums up:

In the Christian understanding, the health of man is a gift from God to be enjoyed by man and employed by him to the glory of God. Health is a quality which extends to the whole of a man's life. It consists of the soundness and wholeness of man's being and of the harmonious integration of function and relationship in all spheres of his body, mind and spirit, which are all inter-related and inter-dependent.

Dr Wilkinson then continues:

The basic relationship of the life of man is that which he bears to God and, since that relationship has been disturbed by man's disobedience and rebellion against God, man has fallen from the high estate in which he was created and lives in a world which has been affected by the consequences of his fall. The result is that complete wholeness or perfect health is not attainable in this world but only in the world which is to come, where sin, disease and death will be no more. Nevertheless health is available to all in this world to an imperfect degree. It is the responsibility of each person to attain and maintain the highest possible level of health in their situation.

Health is manifested by physical growth, fitness, activity, ability and adaptability; by mental maturity, soundness, happiness and creativeness; and by spiritual growth in the grace, knowledge and experience of God. Within society, the health of human beings is reflected in their attitudes to their fellows and in their acceptance of the stewardship of God's creation. It is on these that the well-being of society and the environment depend.

I have quoted Dr Wilkinson and the document he contributed at length because it is the best statement of the ingredients of health that I have seen and I feel it will be helpful to others too. On the basis of it, healing is the restoration of health where it has been impaired. In the Christian context this impairment, brought about by sin, can only be put right through grace. Salvation is the gift of that grace—through Jesus Christ, our Lord.

There is one other concept which I have found useful in the effort to define health, and that is 'harmony'. Harmony is 'a fitting together of parts in order to form a connected whole',[6] and manifestly describes in another way the essence of what I have been trying to present as a concept of whole-ness. It can serve us well as an alternative picture of health—a pun that offers a refreshing and hopeful view of health. Taking in the redemptive element for which I am arguing and which represents that essential element offered by the church's ministry, I suggest that we can usefully think of true health as (to use a phrase introduced earlier) '*holy* harmony'. It is the holiness that makes our wholeness more complete.

Holiness in this context is not the equivalent of moral righteousness. It is that which we can only properly have, if we acknowledge that we cannot possibly have it as a natural part of our being! The only holiness we have or can have is that which we have in and through Christ, We are 'saints' in the very exact sense of that word—people made holy by Christ, people who have no holiness or righteousness of their own.

The gifts of God for our health are these means to healing and wholeness given by a providential Father—the natural healing which doctors forward and indeed others too; 'the leaves of the trees were for the healing of the nations';[7] medical and surgical processes possible through the knowledge that has been given to men and women.

In the end, it is perhaps best to take for oneself the definition that best expresses the positive facets of healthy living. Perhaps balance is a concept that is easy to understand. Perhaps it is the concept of harmony that is helpful. The important, central focus is that which we have now reached in our definition of health as we did in our pleading the case for ministering to the whole person. It confirms us in our commitment to try to help people to be *whole*—physically, mentally, emotionally and spiritually—and to hope that medicine will, as it seems now to be doing, follow that path.

God has given many gifts for our healing and we are free to use them all, preferably together. That he has also given us the gift of redemption and in so doing provided the way back to a right relationship with him, our Maker, is the specifically Christian contribution to the healing spectrum. We leave that element out of ministering to people at our risk—and indeed theirs.

Notes to chapter 5

1–3   I have drawn heavily in chapter 5 on a document written by Dr John Wilkinson for the Church of Scotland's special committee (now discharged) on health and healing. Dr Wilkinson has written a major work on the miracles of healing in the New Testament, *Health and Healing: Studies in New Testament Principles and Practice* (Handsel Press, Edinburgh). It is a most thorough examination of the miracles and is by a doctor–minister. Dr Wilkinson has also written a booklet entitled *Healing and the Church* (Handsel Press, Edinburgh).

4   See chapter 3, p 37
5   See chapter 2, p 32
6   The definition comes from *Chambers Twentieth Century Dictionary*.
7   Revelation 22:2

6

The Healing Community

'On this rock I will build my church'.[1] It was on a response to Peter's confession of Jesus as the Christ that our Lord founded his church. Peter's spiritual awareness and intuition in this declaration 'touched and handled things unseen'.[2]

Such knowledge was not knowledge of the everyday kind, fashioned by the normal processes of the mind. 'Flesh and blood' was not responsible for it, Jesus said. It was revealed knowledge, a revelation from 'my father who is in Heaven'.[3]

This knowledge which 'is beyond knowledge', as Paul describes it,[4] is of a different order from that everyday human knowledge essential to daily living, and survival. When we talk in terms of that Pauline level of knowledge, we are speaking in the language of faith.

It is this which makes it difficult to prove, in a way acceptable and understandable by those who stand outside the faith, the basic Christian beliefs. We are in the realm of a spiritual awareness which is open, in faith, to revelation.

Any such revelation needs, of course, to be objectively tested, such is our capacity for fantasy, imagination and wishful thinking. That objective standard is always there in the Word of God. Our theology must be a *biblical* theology.

That, as I said earlier,[5] has nothing to do with a superficial literalism, but only with our reformation belief in the Word of God as the supreme rule of faith and life, to be read and interpreted under 'the illumination of the Spirit'. It is in moments of raised spiritual awareness that such revelation comes and is received.

The beautiful story of the walk to Emmaus is a marvellous example of such a raising of spiritual awareness.[6] Discussing Jesus of Nazareth on the road with 'the stranger' in attendance, the two disciples did not recognise the Lord. That same evening they did.[7] The normal act of 'breaking bread' at the evening meal became a symbolic act of huge significance.

It is the proper function of a symbol to encourage meaningful associations to flood into our consciousness. Where symbols have ceased to fulfil this function, or have never adequately exercised it, they should be discarded. They simply become—if we are not careful—idolatrous objects. The breaking of the bread, in this story, is a symbolic action that brought back the dramatic events of the Last Supper, the words of Jesus on that occasion and his declamation about the ultimate significance of the death he now faced. For a brief moment the inner capacity to receive revelation was raised, stimulated and illumined. As a result they saw the risen Lord.

I believe the point about the knowledge which is beyond knowledge is important and has relevance for the subject of miracles which I shall discuss in the next chapter.

The foundation on which Jesus built his church was then the confession by Peter of him as 'Christ, the Son of the Living God' (Matt 16:16 *AV*). The continuing basis of the life of the church is that confession, and the acceptance of the Lordship of Christ over his people.

The church must then be for ever obedient to the Lord's commands and instructions.

One of the clearest and most direct of these commands that is given to the church (as I have already said), is to preach the Gospel and heal the sick. Accepting the equal strength of these two instructions—for Jesus does not appear to make any distinction in emphasis in giving them—the church is wholly committed to the healing ministry and to making it a normal part of its life and work. In this sense, the church is called to be the healing community.

How the ministry of healing is to be carried out by the healing community is a matter of interpretation. It is the thrust of this book that (a) the ministry of healing must be taken seriously, and that (b) it must take account of both the specific *command* of Jesus to heal the sick, the clear *example* of Jesus in his expression of his healing ministry, and the implications of the specific instruction he gave to the disciples to proclaim the Good News in words and to express it—the other side of the coin—in compassionate action. His miracles constituted that expression of the Gospel in action and at the same time demonstrated the power of the Kingdom, present in his ministry and, through him 'in his name', in the church he founded to be the healing community.

If this seems, in any way, to be a claim that again hints at arrogance, I hasten to put this in perspective.

The church, which is people—'the people of God', 'the body of Christ'—is made up of sinners. They are no better than others are. They have all the normal human weaknesses and a full share of the shadow side of being.[8] They are subject to all the temptations of the flesh and the spirit—and perhaps particularly vulnerable to the latter in that the desire to be righteous is, if grace is not abundantly present, a breeding-ground for the sins of the spirit. Jesus often declared these to be as bad as, if not worse, than the sins of the flesh. The story of Simon the self-righteous Pharisee who was against the woman who, in love and kindness, washed Jesus' feet with her tears, is one such example.[9] The story of the self-righteous accusers who were against the woman taken in adultery is another.[10] It is not that Christian people are 'better' people. It is simply that they have seen in Christ the one who is Lord and they must be as obedient as they can be, with the help of the Holy Spirit, to his commands—they are under orders.

If then the whole church *is* called to be the healing community, and it is the normal work of the church to express the Gospel in healing ministry, every member of the body of Christ is involved, by virtue of that fact, in the ministry of healing. There is simply no question of those who are interested in this ministry being a clique on the fringe of the church, people who are doing something extra to the normal life of the church. It is the church itself that is the healing body and every member is committed to it.

This important truth is expressed in the way in which, in some congregations, everyone present is involved in the laying on of hands. This practice has long been expressed in Iona Abbey where healing has been an essential part of the Community's witness for many years. Those present gather round in such a way as to make the act a living symbol of the healing community in action.

Some may, however, ask how in fact this principle, so

central to the concept of the healing community, can be realistically worked out in a congregation. I go back to the healing spectrum and take from it *Healing Relationship*. God uses one person to help another to be whole. People are, or can be, one of God's gifts for our healing.

There are many examples of this principle in action in the Bible and I want to use one such situation as the means through which I express the concept of a healing relationship. I cannot refrain from referring, before I do so, to one example of reluctant involvement in a healing relationship and that is the choosing of Ananias to be the person who should minister to St Paul in the trauma of his conversion. Only obedience of a very impressive kind took Ananias to be with the feared Saul of Tarsus of whom he had heard too much![11] His function was clear however. He was to be involved in a healing relationship.

Healing relationship may be expressed in many forms. One expression of it is *friendship* where you seek to encourage wholeness in someone with whom you like to be in relationship, the affection being reciprocated. Then there comes *pastoral care* which is the decision to relate to someone in a helping, caring and therefore healing way. Here we may not be with someone who would be chosen as a friend. The obligation to minister arises out of Christian duty, responsibility and conviction.

Another form of healing relationship is the more formal one—in the sense that it involves structure and contract.[12] It is *pastoral counselling*. This is a discipline for which training is required because a therapeutic relationship can involve the counsellor in coping with unconscious factors[13] —both in himself/herself and in the person to whom ministry is being expressed. The relationship may, for example, include a great deal of 'manipulation' without there being an awareness of this dynamic which is at work in either the counsellor or the client.[14] This can lead to complications as well as being unhelpful to the person in need. In psychotherapy and analytical work, the need for an extended and comprehensive training is imperative, but even in counselling, if it is going to be at any depth at all, it is essential.[15]

All these are healing relationships, but the basic principles of such a relationship apply to them all.

To expound these principles, I direct attention to a familiar New Testament story, that of Jesus and Zacchaeus.[16]

There are three stages in healing relationship and they come out clearly in this incident. First however may I draw attention to a preliminary point of minor importance but which has a purpose.

The first thing Jesus does is to tell Zacchaeus to come down from his perch in the tree into which he has climbed in order to see the Lord, being the little man he [Zacchaeus] was. I do not want to allegorise the story or read into it things not there, but I do see, in this action, the expression of a principle which is important in relationships that set out to be therapeutic, that is healing. People must be on the same level for a relationship to be truly helpful.

There are forms of ministry, for example spiritual direction, where there is a proper element of authority. The trained, experienced director gives advice and directions to the learner/listener. Healing relationship expressed in the form of counselling is of a different order. One, the counsellor, is at the time the person with experience and knowledge. The other is, at the time, the one in need of help. But ten years on, who knows? The counsellor may be the client, and the client may have become a counsellor.

It may be worth mentioning in this context that, in all my experience of counselling training in which I had some responsibility for trainees in this disipline,[17] a large percentage of those now fully involved in counselling were at one time clients. What has happened is that the gain they had made through their experience had provided the essential motivation they felt to offer the same help to others.

Cartoonists, almost without exception, represent marriage guidance and psychotherapeutic situations as an obviously authoritarian official talking down to some poor individual or couple. This is, of course, not what it is like at all. Details, such as ensuring that counsellor and client have similar chairs of the same height and style are important. It must be underlined that healing relationship on a counselling model is, in fact, two people together to see how, by knowledgeable support and loving care, the one in need can be helped to face and deal with 'the problem'. Jesus set aside a 'tree-ground' relationship (that is, at two levels) and in so doing, whether it was intended or not, gave us a reminder of an essential element in healing relationship.

The three main points I want to make—and I apologise for this—are expressed in statements that end with a preposition (and we all know that a preposition is a word we never end a sentence with), but they help this exposition!

1   Healing relationship begins with a movement towards, 'Zacchaeus, I am coming to *your* house today'.

It is a common feature of evangelical campaigns that we make the focus of our effort the bringing of people to where we are. I criticise myself in this because I made the mistake frequently in the parish evangelism I pursued in my charges. If only we could get people to come to the church (we assume) the miracle would happen. Sometimes it did. There are those in the ministry today who were drawn to the church in that way. But when we look at the meaning of 'the church' more closely, we see it as a body of people who, far from summoning others from 'the world' over to their side, in fact move to where people, in their need, are.[18] That place may be an unpleasant one associated with experiences we have never had to undergo and therefore about which we know little, but it is the place from which we have to start. It is the only starting-point for the journey towards wholeness.

This compels us to be careful in our attitudes. There may be, quite appropriately, an element of judgment in spiritual direction. In a healing relationship of the kind I am discussing, we are not there—that is, where that distressed and despairing person is—in a judgmental role. We are not there to condemn ('for God did not send his son into the world to condemn the world, but to save the world through him.'[19]) nor for that matter to condone. His purpose was positive—not to condemn but to save. We have simply, in compassion, moved—as Jesus did with Zacchaeus—towards someone in need. Healing relationship begins with a 'moving towards'.

Theologically this is, of course, entirely sound. The Incarnation is exactly this step, an expression of the compassion of God in his awareness of our need. And so he sent his Son. 'We love, because he first loved us'.[20] In the Incarnation, God moved towards us in Jesus.

2   Healing relationship is expressed in a being with.
The core of this New Testament story is the time Jesus spent 'being with' Zacchaeus.

This particular feature of the story is extemely interesting. Note, for example, that we do not know what Jesus said to Zacchaeus, nor what Zacchaeus said to Jesus. That was a confidential situation and we simply must not invade such a relationship.

I ask you to pause and consider seriously the question of confidentiality in healing relationship. I believe it is a mandatory part of such ministry. The church—that is, its members, and sometimes I am afraid its ministers—does not take confidentiality as seriously as it should. There is on occasion a tendency to talk too easily about members' problems, of whatever kind.

The church has too often a somewhat 'gossipy' feel to it, but this should not be so. In 20 years of participation in leadership rôles in the counselling discipline I have never found confidentiality a problem there. It is, as well as regularly emphasised, taken for granted and is seen to be as binding as medical confidentiality. The church could usefully learn from the example of secular disiplines in this matter.

Confidentiality is, of course, extended to but bounded by the limits of the team, not necessarily only to the individual. If a counsellor or pastoral worker is in a healing relationship and, for any reason, suddenly has to leave—to move house to a distant place, for example—it is very important that whoever takes on that person in need should not have to start at the beginning again, thus compelling a repetition of the whole story. It is essential therefore that confidential casenotes be maintained in regular care or counselling. Most people, when presented with this need, fully understand it. With that caveat about boundaries, individual or team, it is absolutely essential that confidentiality be a normal rule in a helping relationship. If the need to share some fact or facts with a doctor or other appropriate professional arises, it can only be done with permission, and never without it.

It would be beneficial if all involved in pastoral work sought to match the levels of confidentiality that the medical and psychotherapeutic disciplines demand—and get—from their members.

Another minor point, but it is one worth noting for the encouragement of those involved in healing relationships, less formal or highly professional. While Jesus was with Zacchaeus there was, outside his house, a measure of criticism and innuendo. 'The people began to murmur saying that he had gone to be a guest with a man that is a sinner.' It had no effect whatever on the ministry going on inside the house. Whether Jesus was aware of it or not (and, as he 'knew what was in man',[21] he usually sensed what he did not necessarily see or hear), the ministry was neither disturbed nor deflected by it. And so it must be for his servants, similarly involved. There may well be criticism, even innuendo, where there are relationships from which those not involved are rightly excluded, but so long as the 'ministering persons' know what they are doing and why they are doing it, there is no need for concern of any kind.[22] But because an intimate relationship of a therapeutic kind involves risk, a real degree of self-awareness is essential for those who are working in healing relationships.[23]

I return to the theme of 'being with' because it is of the essence of healing relationship. The text for such ministry is in effect in Ezekiel: 'I sat where they sat'.[24] You cannot help people in distress, despair, or devastation by suggesting, in any way at all, that they should never have got themselves into such a position. There is no comfort as well as no help in such statements, suggestions or hints. They are where they are. That is the fact of life. The counsellor (I use this word, and the other word, client, in a general sense at this point to cover all ministry of the kind we are discussing) having moved—in compassion—to where the suffering client is, must be with them there. It is only from that point that healing can begin. It takes account of the facts, and it encourages acceptance of these facts and some realisation of how the whole situation may have come about. The source may be related to personal history, personality development, 'learned responses' to situations, hereditary end environmental factors, and so on. (That is a huge area into which we cannot go here.[25]) It then looks for the new direction in which healing lies. This, in terms of healing relationships which are explicitly Christian in their approach, will involve the means of grace—prayer, faith, forgiveness, and so on.

A word of caution may be appropriate here. Obviously healing relationship involves sympathy and, even more, empathy. Though it can be difficult to empathise with situations involving behaviour and practices quite outside our experience, it is imperative that we are unshockable in the face of, say, sordid material, perversion and interpersonal violence. By unshockable I do not for one moment mean that we should be so used to the unpleasantness of life that we become hardened to it. We must always be aware of the risk of allowing the 'hardened heart' to come about, for it speaks of insensitivity and that loss of 'feel' for the good and lovely that constitute a Christian virtue. I refer rather to the ability not to be thrown by the stories which are presented. In a healing relationship there must be the ability to accept all that is brought by the damaged person to whom we are seeking to minister, because it is part of their life, a part they have to own.

There is a very important principle here. The compassion which compels us to move towards people in despair and which demands that we are with them wherever they are, involves the ability to accept another, 'warts and all'. There is no great difficulty receiving the good things people bring. The crunch lies in finding the way to accept the negative or shadow side, the unacceptable side, of an individual.[26] To achieve this, there are two things we must do. The *first* is to learn the ability to accept the negative, unacceptable side of *ourselves*—a very demanding task. And, *second*, is to realise that we are bound to accept others 'warts and all' because it is exactly this that God has done for us in Christ. He loves not simply the good points we bring; he accepts us in our totality and that means all that is good and all that is bad together. Indeed this is the glory of the Gospel and the grandeur of the doctrine of grace.

I emphasised empathy as an essential attitude in 'being with' people, and rightly so, but there must be a word of warning here about how we express empathy. We simply must not say 'I know how you feel', because we cannot know the feelings of another. If we have been through a similar situation, we can empathise to a degree but no two situations are exactly the same.

Recently, I was invited to talk to over 100 parents who had one thing in common and that is that they had all lost a child through death.[27] It may have been through sudden or long-term illness, an accident, murder or suicide. I have not lost a child through death. I nearly did, but that child in fact survived critical illness. It is an arrogance and an impertinence for me to say to such a gathering of people, many recently bereaved and still feeling their loss acutely. 'I know how you feel'. I cannot know that, however hard I try to do so.

This kind of sensitivity is essential in a healing relationship. The cliché, pious or otherwise, is a dangerous form of expression. We must indeed be careful in the use of words for they do imply attitudes. People in need are sensitive to the way others look at their unhappy situations. We will not forward the healing process if in our endeavour to do it, deliberately or accidentally, we add to hurt.

I have felt it right to stay for some time with the concept I am describing as 'a being with'. It is what Jesus offered Zacchaeus. It is at the heart of healing.

Once again, theologically, this is essential Christianity. The Incarnation is the step God took to be with us. Indeed, one of the New Testament names of Jesus is given as *Immanuel*, which means 'God with us'. So Jesus came to share the pain of the world, to encounter the despair of the world, to be with the desperate whatever has led to their descent into hell. That Jesus himself, between Crucifixion and Resurrection, descended into hell may produce various explanations, some perhaps of a psychic kind, but the significance of such an act lies for me in his being willing to go to the lowest depths to be with those caught in those depths. At the heart of the Gospel, there is a 'being with'.

3   The third element in a healing relationship is the 'going on'—or in the language of counselling, growth.

Where there has been a 'moving towards' and a 'being with', such as that demonstrated in the Zacchaeus story, there follows growth. We do not know, as I said before, what Jesus said to Zacchaeus or Zacchaeus to Jesus, but we do know the result. Zacchaeus shows that he has set out on the road to wholeness by the things he is now determined to do—that is put right injustice, offer help to the needy, and so on.

It is in the same way that we shall see the results of our healing relationships expressed, in change; changed ways, changed attitudes, a changed direction. Nothing can be more satisfying than that. There is therefore a splendid corollary to engagement in a healing relationship. Not only do we find change is taking place in the other, what is significant is that we ourselves grow through the process.

It is this added blessing that most surely comes to those who undertake this form of healing ministry and thus contribute to another's health. It often leads to people undertaking such ministry as a life-work. Through it we are indeed ourselves made more whole. To be engaged in work that carries such an added benefit is blessing indeed.

Notes to Chapter 6

1   Matthew 16:18
2   See Introduction, note 2.
3   Matthew 16:17
4   See Introduction, note 4.
5   See chapter 1.
6   Luke 24:1–35
7   Luke 24:31
8   The 'shadow' is discussed in chapter 9, on the Unconscious.
9   Luke 7:36–50
10   John 8:1–11. The authenticity of this story in textual terms has been questioned, but it does have, as in a favoured J B Phillips phrase, the 'ring of truth'.
11   Acts 9:10–22
12   'Contract' is used as a technical term to describe the nature of

the agreement and commitment between counsellor and client in a therapeutic relationship.

13   Chapter 9 will discuss matters relating to the unconscious.

14   See note 13 above.

15   The difference between counselling, psychotherapy and analysis relates mainly to the depth or level at which the work is done.

16   Luke 19:1–10

17   In particularly, the seven years as Training Supervisor at Westminster Pastoral Foundation, as already mentioned.

18   I recall Bernard Braley, a Methodist layman who specialised in the development of new ways of worship, on several conference occasions dividing an audience (of about 20 people) into those who were to be the church and went to one side of the room, and those who were to be 'the world outside' and were sent to the other side. The church people were then asked to make contact with 'the world'—*non*-verbally only. They immediately made gestures inviting 'the world' to come and join them. This, of course, Mr Braley expected would always happen—and it did! It gave him the opportunity to make his point about the real nature of evangelism—the church going *to* the world and not the other way round. Mr Braley was Managing Director of Stainer and Bell Ltd, and is the publisher of many books associated with the name Galliard (an imprint within Stainer & Bell) on contemporary ministry.

19   John 3:17

20   I John 4:19

21   John 2:25

22   'Ministering persons' is a phrase John Sanford uses for all engaged in pastoral work, whether ordained or lay, in his book *Ministry Burnout* (Arthur James, 1984).

23   Chapter 9, on The Unconscious, will underline this statement.

24   Ezekiel 3:15, *Authorised Version*

25   The whole field of 'development of personality' is important for the study of adult problems.

26   The 'unacceptable side' will be discussed in chapter 9.

27   The Compassionate Friends is a national self-help support organisation for bereaved parents. This national body has its offices at 6 Denmark Street, Bristol BS1 5DQ. Tel: 0272 292 778.

7

The Mystery of Suffering

There are two concepts which it is essential that we hold together as we seek to look at the ministry of healing. One is that of 'miracle' and the other is what I call 'the mystery of suffering'. In the healing ministry, both of these concepts are important.

Let me begin with miracle and immediately state that the Christian faith is, in my view, committed to a belief in the miraculous. It all depends, of course, on the definition we give of the word miracle—and a whole book could be written on that theme! I see miracle as follows.

Miracles are, essentially, 'divine surprises', things which happen which cannot, in terms of our present knowledge, be explained in logical, rational, intellectual terms. They do not contradict laws that we know. They are simply not able to be described in words and concepts we normally use to express our thoughts. In other words, I go back to that phrase used earlier—it came from a profound passage in Ephesians— such concepts belong to the knowledge which 'is beyond knowledge'.[1] As we found it to be true in the case of Peter's confession, we are not here in the realm of ordinary human knowledge. We are in the realm of faith with its higher level of knowledge—the knowledge that is beyond knowledge.

There is a tendency in Christian circles to argue for a concept of miracle that involves 'intervention'. I do not set this word wholly aside for I see it as referring—to recall Paul Tillich's phrase—'to the divine activity of the Holy Spirit'.[2] It does however perhaps suggest a God who 'steps in' and does something different from, or even contrary to, his own laws. And that can be misleading.

Christopher Hamel Cooke, in his book *Health is for God*,[3] has argued against the use of the word 'intervention' and talks rather of God's 'continuing creation'. There is value in this emphasis and it is one that much appeals to some thinkers. It underlines what I feel I am presenting as the miraculous, namely things which happen as a consequence of the creative activity of God. For his ways are not in conflict with, but beyond, our understanding. In other words, there are principles—spriritual laws—at work and these laws involve examples of creative activity that we cannot explain. What we can do and must do is accept them in faith. They belong to the realm of the knowledge which is beyond knowledge.

If this concept of miracle is valid, then the Christian faith is itself founded on miracle. The Incarnation, the Resurrection, the Ascension, the coming of the Holy Spirit—these are all miracles. They cannot be explained in terms of ordinary knowledge. They belong to the knowledge which is beyond knowledge. They are however accepted and believed by faith. Can we therefore do anything other than say, God being God, and the Holy Spirit being the divine activity of God in the world, that there will be no more 'divine surprises'? I think not.

The realm of healing, from time to time, throws up miracles, cases of people being healed physically and in other ways, in circumstances that cannot be explained in terms of ordinary human knowledge.

In 1986, with the help of professional colleagues, we produced a video on *The Healing Ministry*.[4] In it we presented the cases of Russell and Carolyn. Russell's sight was miraculously restored following the laying on of hands after he lost his field of vision in a photocopier accident. Ten years ago Carolyn was in a wheelchair, very seriously ill with multiple sclerosis. She stood up and walked after prayer and the laying on of hands and has walked normally ever since.

I do not argue these cases. They are simply presented in their own right as facts of life. 'Once I was blind—indeed a few minutes ago. Now I can see', Russell, a schoolmaster, would say. Carolyn would testify to her healing, but sees the physical cure as only part and, she would emphasise, a not too important part of it. That is not a sign of ingratitude for that physical healing, but a statement of the greater importance of wholeness, a wholeness to which she moved through what happened to her.

There are many more who can testify to similar events, operations that never took place (a nun who had x-rays showing the need for a lung operation who, after the laying on of hands, had a further x-ray and the condition had gone.[5] The operation, due over a decade ago, has never taken place), conditions that disappeared (like an eye condition that vanished and so surprised the ophthalmic surgeon that he produced photographs of 'before and after' and presented them to the one who had given healing ministry in Jesus' name).[6] There will be more surprises in a world in which God is at work in history, personal and corporate, and where 'the Spirit bloweth where it listeth'.

For such miraculous happenings, we all want to 'praise the Lord', and do. The agony is on the other side of the equation for, clearly and obviously, for every miracle that happens, so many more do not—certainly in the way for which prayers were asked. Yes, of course, there may be healing of a different kind at another level. Of course, as I shall shortly claim, there is a healing through suffering that is enormously impressive. There is also even a phrase, quite properly used to make an important point, 'a healing through dying'.[7] All these things are true (although the critics of this ministry sometimes feel we are in a situation in which we can claim healing, whatever happens). What I am concerned to put before you now is the reality of suffering. The healing ministry *must* take account of the mystery of suffering and never paint a picture of endless healings, unsubstantiated generalisations, unexamined cases that can bring the ministry into disrepute. It is sadly a widespread fault particularly in healing circles outside the church to make such claims but it happens in Christian organisations too. It is totally wrong in integrity terms. Additionally, it does not help in developing medical-religious understanding. Nothing makes doctors so impatient with healing ministry as the kind of claims that are virtually groundless and to them (as indeed to us all) unreal.

The problem of suffering remains the most difficult problem within the Christian purview. The critics can point to the ghastly disasters, like the Zeebrugge tragedy and say 'Where is your God?'. They can point to the crippling illnesses that afflict mankind and ask how a God of love can allow such things to happen. They can ask about the earthquakes, land-slides and other natural disasters. Involvement in the healing ministry compels those who seek to be channels of the healing power of the Risen Christ to be totally realistic about the mystery of suffering. It remains the so-called '$64 000 question', the full implications of which lie beyond our reach. We see 'in part only' and not in terms of the full picture as God sees it. We can only 'see through a glass darkly' and not 'face to face'.

I think of two ladies I knew a decade ago. They were both in the same age group; they were both articulate and able people; they both were ill. The diagnosis was terminal cancer, with a year given as the probable time during which they could continue to work. Both had the best available medical treatment, both had much prayer, both had laying on of hands. One is alive today and as busy as ever. The other had to endure an appalling year and died soon after the year was up. It is a situation in which one can only take out of its context a sentence from the New Testament and apply it here: 'One is taken and another is left'. We do not know why. We must always ask 'What does this mean?'. On one hand, we have the miracle (and whether the medicine accomplished it, or the prayers, or the laying on of hands, or all three, is irrelevant, for all these things are, in terms of my healing spectrum, the gifts of God). On the other side, the miracle just does not happen. Were there 'blocks' (to use psychological jargon)? Was there a self-destructive syndrome at work be-cause of guilt (which was very present in the lady who died, on two grounds which for confidentiality reasons I cannot state)? Did the lady who died not really want to be well? I cannot answer these questions although they are all in my mind. I am simply faced here with what I can only call the mystery of suffering. It remains just that.

It is not the purpose of this book to try to answer the ultimate questions about the meaning of suffering, but it is a theme which the healing ministry has to take very seriously.

Suffering brings two questions to which there are no final answers. One is, 'Why does this happen to me?'. That is part of the mystery of suffering. The other is, 'Why is there suffer-ing at all, and suffering so appalling, when God is said to be love?'. There, too, is mystery. It is not possible with intellectual argument to deal properly with the feelings of the bereaved. Whatever I say may help some, but will irritate, annoy, even infuriate others. All I seek to do is, looking at the questions in relation to the healing ministry, set down glimpses of light that *may* illuminate something for someone in a very dark area.

The first insight I take from the Bible as a whole, and the Genesis stories in particular. The Bible is the exposition of the human dilemma and offers the answer to it. The world which God made good[8] is a good thing spoiled.[9] The damage is caused by deliberate disobedience[10] in the face of special commands.[11] As a result, human nature becomes 'fallen' or corrupt, and every part of it—mind, body, imagination, will— is affected. It is not 'total corruption' as some theologians of another age saw it, but a corruption which affects every part of us. The capacity to respond to the good remains, but the imbalance is reflected in the much greater compulsion to do evil. That condition is dramatically described by St Paul in Romans chapter 7 when he confesses to be aware of 'a law in my members' that 'when I would do good, evil is present with me'. And so Paul expresses the very essence of the human dilemma, the dilemma of a fallen humanity, 'The good that I would, I do not. The evil that I would not, that I do'. The cry at the end of this confession is one of desperation—'Who will deliver me from the body of this death?'[12]

The New Testament contains God's answer to this dilemma, as does St Paul's same letter, 'I thank God, through Jesus Christ'. The Gospel is the Good News of the grace which is on offer to those who will respond. This is salvation.

In the Genesis story, the results of man's disobedience are listed. To the woman, he said:

> I will increase your labour and your groaning,
> and in labour you shall bear children.
> You shall be eager for your husband,
> and he shall be your master.

Genesis 3:16

To the man, he said, in verse 17

Because you have listened to your wife
and have eaten from the tree which I forbade you,
accursed shall be the ground on your account.
With labour you shall win your food from it
all the days of your life.
It will grow thorns and thistles for you,
none but wild plants for you to eat.
You shall gain your bread by the sweat of your brow
until you return to the ground;
for from it you were taken.
Dust you are, to dust you shall return.

New English Bible

Suffering is not something 'sent' by God. It is part of a world affected by sin. The choices which are made by human beings often abuse God's gifts. There is a general link between sin and suffering.[13] They are products of a world in which humanity has genuine freedom and real free will, but that freedom is abused. The choice ultimately is between a world wholly controlled by a puppeteer called God, and one which is truly free. The latter is the one that exists—'for better or for worse' (and all would surely say for better). The risk is the abuse of that freedom, the cost is expressed in suffering.

The second glimpse of light is the making clear—and again this is done on the basis of the Bible's witness—that while there is a general connection between sin and suffering at the roots of our troubled world, making particular links is very dangerous. Jesus says this specifically and clearly. The passage is in Luke 13:1–5:

There were present at that season some that told him of the Galileans, whose blood Pilate had mingled with their sacrifices.

And Jesus, answering, said unto them, suppose ye that these Galileans were sinners above all the Galileans, because they suffered such things?

I tell you, Nay: but except ye repent, ye shall all likewise perish.

Or those eighteen, upon whom the tower in Siloam fell, and slew them, think ye that they were sinners above all men that dwelt in Jerusalem?

> I tell you, Nay: but, except ye repent, ye shall all likewise perish.
>
> *Authorised Version*

The message is clear. We cannot relate suffering directly and quantitively to sin. We are all sinners. We all deserve punishment, but suffering is not meted out on that basis. Were those who died in the Zeebrugge disaster greater sinners than others? We know such a statement to be nonsense. However suffering affects people and whoever suffers, it remains a mystery. What cannot be assumed is that specific suffering relates to specific sin when we are faced with the tragedies and disasters of life. Of course it can be true. Promiscuity may well lead to disease, as the AIDS problem shows, but the innocent are victims too, children who cannot possibly have any responsibility for their parents' behaviour. So it is with others who are victims—those who have received affected blood, for example.

Jesus, of course, came across those who dealt with the problem of suffering in this wrong way. 'Who did sin, this man or his parents?', he was asked—and it was by his disciples—when faced by a man who was blind. There must be such a link, they implied, but Jesus' answer is again clear. Neither the blind man nor his parents had sinned.[14]

Thus the mystery of suffering goes on. The innocent suffer and the evil do not get their just deserts.

The third glimpse of light on this whole problem is the particular example of that last statement, that the innocent suffer, for did not the sinless Son of God suffer the most horrifying death of crucifixion and all that went with it? I have only to state this to begin to show that the clues to the answer to the mystery of suffering go much deeper. The context in which Jesus saw his Messiahship was that of the innocent Suffering Servant, despised, rejected, a man of sorrows and acquainted with grief.[15] Suffering was at its most acute where it was least deserved. So the mystery of suffering, with its injustice remains. What more is there to say about it? I think just one thing which again I will not argue intellectually for *I* have no right to make the point. I offer the testimony of real people, and it is in this testimony that the *positive* relationship (I repeat that I quote those who have suffered or are suffering) between suffering and healing is demonstrated.

In the video on *The Healing Ministry* to which I referred earlier, we tell the story of Lin. Because it is all there to be seen and heard, the story is a public one, and I am thankfully not bound by confidentiality over it. I say 'thankfully' because Lin's story has moved many, and it ought to be told as an encouragement.

I met Lin some years ago when she came into my care as a student in counselling training in the Westminster Pastoral Foundation. She spent one full-time year and two part-time years with us. She was a telephone switchboard operator, and later training supervisor, in a City bank.

Sometime later, in 1985, Lin rang me up. I had seen her *en passant* once since she had left our training centre. Now she was ringing to ask if she could do more training—had I suggestions to make about what she could do?

We discussed this in detail, and then I asked her what other things she was doing. She had given up her switchboard work because she was so busy with other things. She had set up a bereavement counselling unit. She was giving special attention to the problems of the disabled, especially in sexual matters. She was writing her second book. She was training to be a lay preacher and hopefully beyond that, to enter the ministry. It was a full life indeed, but you may feel you know of others as heavily committed.

There is, however, more to tell about Lin. When she was born, prematurely, a medical accident involving the use of oxygen took place. As a result, Lin was cerebrally palsied. She did not have the use of the lower part of her body. At the age of 13, after years of intensive physiotherapy and operations on her legs, she was able to take her first steps. She has been able to get about to some extent on level surfaces with the help of her tripod sticks, but otherwise has to go everywhere in a wheelchair or by taxi.

When Lin was nine, she lost the sight of one eye—as a further consequence of that medical error—and at 14 she had a detached retina in the other, 'good' eye. An operation to deal with that condition was unsuccessful and Lin has been blind since then.

It is in the light of all this—cerebrally palsied and blind—that her record represents 'the magnificence of suffering'. Consider the list of her achievements just mentioned: writing, counselling, teaching, preaching and training.

It is an incredible list—and there will be more to add to it. What is relevant to the theme is Lin's statement that 'the best things that have happened to me in terms of service have all taken place since I became blind'. The journey has taken Lin *through* suffering to wholeness.

This, too, is the healing ministry at work. The physical miracles may not be possible—as Lin knows—but the road to wholeness sometimes does pass through suffering, and in doing so produces magnificent results.

Lin's testimony is borne out by others who have suffered greatly. It may be wholly outside any possibility for us as ordinary people to be able to see in extreme pain an opportunity to 'share in the suffering of our Lord'.[16] It takes someone far along the road to wholeness to express the healing ministry in such a way. What perhaps we can understand, even though it lies outside our own experience, is the moving tribute of the husband and wife who both found they had terminal cancer, but lived on beyond their medically estimated time:

> 'We do not know whether we have been cured of our cancers, but we do know that through the whole experience we are much more whole than we ever were before.'

Within that glorious statement there is in essence the true meaning of healing.

Notes to Chapter 7

1 Ephesians 3:19, *New English Bible*
2 See Chapter 1, note 33.
3 Christopher Hamel Cooke, *Health is for God* (Arthur James, 1986)
4 Available on sale or hire from The Churches' Council for Health and Healing, St Marylebone Parish Church, Marylebone Road, London NW1 5LT. There are two versions—46 minutes and 37 minutes, VHS and Betamax (longer version only).

5 I refer to attested cases of healing and repeat my warning about vague presentations.
6 This case is recorded by George Fox of the Divine Healing Fellowship, in Scotland, and I have seen the photographs.
7 A moving book on this theme is by Saxon Walker, *Sheila—a healing through dying* (Arthur James, 1986).
8 Genesis, chapter 1
9 Genesis, chapter 3
10 Genesis 3:6
11 Genesis 2:16–17
12 Romans 7:15–25
13 They are both products of a 'fallen' world.
14 John 9:3
15 Isaiah, chapter 53
16 I am much aware, as I write this, of a Roman Catholic nun I know well who has seen a miracle—I referred to her in that context earlier—but who also has to endure severe pain and has had to do so for many years. It is she who sees her suffering and pain in this way.

8

Simplicity and Over-Simplification

There are two more concepts that need to be held together as we look at matters of health and healing. The first is 'simplicity' and the second is 'over-simplification'.

The Christian faith is, essentially, a simple faith. I do *not* mean by simple that it is naïve or simplistic. I mean that we Christians should have a much greater faith than we normally do.

In an earlier chapter, I mentioned the story of the walk to Emmaus and the irony of the fact that—although the two disciples were discussing Jesus of Nazareth—they were at the same time totally unaware that he was there.[1] The subject of their theological discussion was there beside them! This I pointed out was a cautionary tale, one that draws attention to the danger of purely mental involvement in the faith.

I also want to underline once more that, in pointing out that theoretical discussion may actually blind us to spiritual reality, I am far from denying the need for theology or discrediting the discipline. I would indeed take precisely the opposite point of view. We need more good theology not less, especially in relation to the ministry of healing. We need major theological work that demonstrates the necessity for the ministry to be taken seriously. That work has not yet been done and this is not the book in which it should be attempted because (a) the purpose of this book is to stimulate understanding of Christ's healing ministry at a more popular level, and (b) I do not have the competence necessary to undertake such a task. That there is no major theological work of the required academic level is something I may play a part in seeking to correct, but in an enabling role only![2] I believe the healing ministry to be of the essence of the church's witness and that the great doctrines of the Incarnation, the

Resurrection, the Holy Spirit, the Church, the Atonement, justification and sanctification, salvation and grace are all part of the foundations of this ministry. I believe above all that the Christian doctrine of forgiveness is of crucial importance to healing, and I shall try to say something on that in a later chapter.[3] My plea therefore for a simple faith has to be seen against that background.

The simple faith for which I want to argue is founded on the need to take Jesus at his word much more than we do. He spoke with authority. He is the authority on the spiritual life. He was aware of the immense spiritual power represented in himself as Messiah. We cannot be Christ, nor get within a million miles of such a possibility, but it was his promise to the disciples that they would 'receive power, after that the Holy Ghost is come upon you'.[4]

It was that kind of promise, borne out in due course by events, that led him to encourage expectation. 'If you have faith as a grain of mustard seed, you shall say to this mountain Move hence to yonder place'.[5] That statement needs to be analysed and understood. Notice that he does not ask for 'quantity' in faith (a mustard seed is tiny). He asks for the reality of faith. In many instances he talks of the faith that has made people whole.[6] In an extraordinary statement to the disciples in John's Gospel, he tells them they shall do yet 'greater works'.[7] We, in our limited human understanding see only the tip of the iceberg of the full resources of the Spirit. They are infinitely greater than we can imagine. The possibility of miracle, in the sense in which I have defined it, is restricted by our limited faith and lack of expectation. This, the true simplicity of Christian faith, is a difficult point to make because it is open to very dangerous misunderstandings. These lie in the realms of faith and expectation.

The healing ministry is often described as 'faith-healing' and understandably so—in one sense. The element of faith was so much present in the miracle stories of the Gospels and received such emphasis and admiration from Jesus that we must take account of it.[8] The practical danger, given that we are but weak human beings and not Christ, is that it is all too easy to believe that if you have *enough* faith, you will be healed. In other words, contrary to my point about the mustard seed above, *quantity* is felt to count. The corollary is that when people thus believing are not healed, they must assume that they did not have enough faith.

Human history is littered with the tragedies that come from that misunderstanding. They include not just, if I might so describe them, 'blind' believers, but very thoughtful, mature and deeply spiritual people.

We are then back with the mystery of suffering and all the questions that come when people who have, and show, faith are not healed. This dilemma is the apparent contradiction that there is on the one hand in the encouragement to people—and it is a biblically-based encouragement—to have a much more simple faith in the remarkable resources of God, but on the other hand, the warning that must be given over unrealistic expectation. It is not easy to find the proper balance in relation to this paradox.

We have already discussed, by implication, some of the reasons for physical cures not taking place—for example the inner resistance that is expressed in a desire for healing when in fact at the deeper levels, we may not really want to be well.[9] There is the example of Paul and his 'thorn . . . in the flesh',[10] where he prayed three times for a cure but it was not given.[11] Was it that he had more to learn through his affliction before he had release from it? Is, generalising that question, one of the functions of suffering, the need to grow through it?[12] Is it that, wholeness being the Christian's aim (rather than cure), there is, in some shape and sense, a need for us to face extra suffering? Is it that illness is often a much more complicated conditon than we realise and that the causes of it lie deeper than we imagine? (To that last question I will turn later.) These are all questions that are very difficult to answer. Indeed, given the element of mystery brought about by the dark glass through which we human beings have to look,[13] they may be questions that are impossible to answer. But they all relate to the disappointments that arise through a misunderstanding of the role of faith in healing.

It is worth spending a moment looking at just that.

It is our understanding of the Sacraments, whether our tradition be that of the two dominical sacraments or the wider seven of some theological traditions,[14] that the efficacy of a

Sacrament lies not in the work of the one who ministers or celebrates, but in a conjunction of several factors—the divine promises associated with the sacraments (and this, for me, makes 'proclamation' essential to a Eucharist or Holy Communion), the use of the appointed elements and the presence of faith in the recipient. Without that last element, the sacraments become simply magic. Faith in this context is response. It is the 'Amen' on being served the bread and the wine in the Lord's Supper, a saying 'yes' to God and his offered grace. Jesus asks in the narrative about the miracle by the temple pool which I have already discussed, 'Wilt thou be made whole?' (John 5:6, *AV*). Healing is a co-operative matter effected with us and through us, rather than superimposed upon us.[15]

We must note that the faith can also be on behalf of another. The centurion's faith saves his servant.[16] The faith of Mary and Martha plays a part in Lazarus coming back to life.[17] It is the presence of the element of faith that is so essential and it must be provided by somebody. It can of course be the faith of the praying body or the healing community. The church may provide the element of faith needed for the blessing of people.

The use of the word faith-healing tends to be discouraged in Christian healing ministry circles because of the danger of its misleading ill people by creating false expectations. There is a need within the healing ministry for that sense of responsibility which all Christians must show, but never in such a way that we hide the necessity of the church expecting great things of God. For this reason, the healing ministry must always be preceded by teaching. The forwarding of the ministry in a congregation must be founded on consistent teaching. The ministry must never, in any way, give an appearance of magic. The simple faith I am suggesting is based solely and wholly on the need to *believe* Jesus' words, and in some way to act on them. We must never mislead people or raise false expectations, but we must somehow convey that the divine promises are so much greater than our limited understanding of them.

The other side of this equation is the danger of over-simplification in interpreting illness. To fall into this trap is to be irresponsible too.

I have already referred to the common practice of some so-called 'healers' and, as I said then, of some within the Christian ministry of healing too, who enthusiastically and sincerely generalise an illness and its cure, be it physical or mental.[18] This does, I fear, happen in some approaches to The Healing of the Memories, a concept which will arise as we go on. Illness can be very complex. In discussing the matter here, I point to two reasons for offering this warning. They are related reasons, but the second one brings in a major new factor and to that I will have to give extended consideration, hence its being the subject of the next chapter.

Illness can be complicated just because it is not caused by purely physical factors. If there is an inter-relationship between the physical, the emotional, the mental and the spiritual, dis-ease in any one part of our being may produce, or condition, the possibility of disease in another area.

This brings whole new elements into the understanding of illness. We are no longer dealing with viruses and other physical causes of illness only. We are no longer in the realm of wholly measurable elements in illness. We are now looking for reasons other than those physical ones that can explain someone's persistent illness or illnesses.

This is no longer the world of the test-tube and the thermometer, however necessary these things are. It is a world in which the doctor is the layman and has no special knowledge just because he is a doctor. He/she is not by virtue of his/her medical training a trained therapist. It is a world in which, for example, attitudes and moods must be taken into account.

The question of moods is an important one, for it is manifestly clear that our moods condition our 'well-being'. Feelings of confidence and competence can easily be destroyed by the arrival of someone we do not like (which really means who threatens us) and in a moment our present mood can change totally. With that change, our sense of well-being goes too. We may feel ill as a result of such an experience. The sky goes dark, the future feels grim, there is little right with the world and we long for 'the good old days, when people were nice and everything was so much better'. As the dismal seems to dominate, and the clouds gather ominously, we can very easily become ill.

An examination of our mood-swings, noting when and in what circumstances these occur, may well offer clues to the self-aware as to why they are feeling unwell or indeed as to how their illness is developing.

It is also worth noting that one of the ways in which psychological and spiritual factors contribute to health is in their ability to shape our attitudes. Paul's comment that he had 'learned in whatsoever state' he was 'therein to be content' is not a statement about resignation.[19] It is rather a declaration of attitudes which enable him to gain through circumstances rather than to be submerged by them. The *New English Bible*'s translation of this sentence points to the positive element when Paul says 'I have learned to find resources within myself whatever the circumstance, I triumph still'.[20]

It is the presence and influence of psychosomatic factors that may contribute to the way illness may develop or recovery may take place. On the positive side, this argues strongly for the creation and upbuilding of a faith as an aid to health and healing. On the negative side the part played by emotional and spiritual elements in the complex interrelationship between mind, soul and body may make the causes of ill-health difficult to determine. It certainly is dangerous to over-simplify some illnesses and talk all too superficially and irresponsibly about healing where healing as yet clearly has not come.

This takes us on to the second and very specific related factor in illness. It continues the theme of the presence of elements other than purely physical ones in the creation of illness. Because it is such an important subject, I now devote major consideration specifically to it. I am in fact talking of what is known, in psychological language, as 'the unconscious'.

Notes to Chapter 8

1 See chapter 6, pp 62–63
2 Initial steps have been taken to bring this about, but cannot, at this stage, be mentioned in detail.
3 See chapter 11.
4 Acts 1:8, *Authorised Version*

5   Matthew 17:20
6   For example, see Luke 7:50 and Mark 5:34 *et al.*
7   John 14:12
8   For example, see Luke 7:9.
9   John 5:1–18, AV
10   II Corinthians 12:7
11   II Corinthians 12:8
12   II Corinthians 12:9–10
13   I Corinthians 13:12
14   The difference in the number of sacraments does not affect the point made.
15   See chapter 11, pp 113–114
16   Luke 7:1–10
17   John 11:1–46
18   It is an unhappy experience when one is faced by a manifest lack of change in people whose cases have been publicly proclaimed as examples of healing.
19   Philippians 4:11
20   The phrase comes from the hymn *Abide with me* by Henry Francis Lyte.

9

The Unconscious

There are four kinds of knowledge about ourselves which we can identify. There is, *first*, the knowledge we have of ourselves and which others have of us. This is fairly superficial knowledge, but it is real and must be acknowledged.

There is, *second*, the knowledge that we have of ourselves which we are not prepared to share with others, unless they be intimate friends, family or counsellors. How far we are willing to do that will vary from person to person. Our unwillingness to share this knowledge is our shame over it! We like, understandably, to present ourselves as kind, considerate, thoughtful, well-behaved people. We know, of course, that the reality is different. There is a negative side to us too of which we are (or ought to be) very aware. We keep this knowledge to ourselves.

The *third* kind of knowledge is that which others have of us, but we do not have of ourselves. It is well summed up by Robert Burns in his famous words: 'O wad some Pow'r the giftie gie us, To see oursels as others see us!' (*To a Louse*).

This is an important area of knowledge and one to which we must always give serious consideration. We do not always realise just how we come across to other people.

I recall, some years ago, being in Switzerland at an international conference on pastoral care and conselling. Part of the programme determined that we should be in small groups so we met six times during the conference in that way. The group in which I was placed was made up (as I remember) of two Americans, two East Germans, one Finnish female social worker, two Scots, one Indian and one West German. Our leader was a distinguished American father-figure in the pastoral counselling discipline.

When we came to the final two meetings, our leader decided

that we must participate in an exercise which consisted of asking one of our group to take his/her chair into a corner of the room and face the wall. The process would be repeated over the two sessions by each in turn. The group would then close up and proceed to discuss that member of it as if he or she were not there, especially looking at the way he/she had presented him- or herself to the whole group.

This is not an exercise I would recommend for the average church meeting of whatever kind—at least not without giving it considerable thought beforehand! It does however have benefits, some pleasant and some painful. You did hear re-affirming statements and that is always encouraging. You did also hear surprising things of a negative kind, ways in which you had come across, ways which may have irritated or even stirred up anger.

It is important that, in the interests of greater self-awareness, we take account of the knowledge which others have of us, but which we do not ourselves have. It need not be treated as revealed truth, for the commentators may have problems of their own which are contributing to their perceptions of us, but it is certainly wise to consider what is being said about us. There may be things we ought to change in our self-presentation.

Here then are three areas of knowledge about us, what we have and share, what we have but are unwilling to share, and what others have of us but we may not have of ourselves. There is however the crucial *fourth* area and that is the know-ledge others do not have of us and we do not have of our-selves. It is in this area of our being which is called by the psychologists 'The Unconscious'.

It is not the purpose of this book to give a technical descrip-tion of that whole area which is popularly described as 'sub-conscious'. That belongs to psychological and—as I believe—spiritual manuals. My concern here is to try to give some understanding of the factors which may be involved in making us ill and especially those which complicate the causes and development of our illnesses. I will therefore try to explain the essence of this concept, recognising at the same time that it may all be wholly familiar to many readers. I hope too to point up the subtlety of the way in which our unconscious can act. It is deep in the area of the hidden memories that so much that is disruptive lies. The wiles of the unconscious area of our being are famous and infamous. It is the source of our unacknowledged manipulation of people, to our own ends—(there is a clue to one possible purpose of illness here). But it is also important to stress that it is the fount of creativity too.

This is, in fact, an important point about the unconscious. While we will have to look at the negative or shadow side of the unconscious—for it is the real trouble-maker—it is very necessary to establish that that area of our being is constructive-creative as well as, in the sense in which I am using the word, destructive. It is from the unconscious that music, poetry, painting and all the wonder of the creative arts come. Ask an artist from where his/her images and concepts come and the answer will point to unknown areas within. What is the source of beautiful compositions, glorious harmony of the kind which touches the human heart, and the answer may well be along the lines of 'I don't really know. Something inside me ...'. The unconscious is the place of creation through which the Spirit can work. 'Deep calls to deep'.[2] The Spirit speaks with our spirit.[3] It is the place of creative meeting and from that encounter good will surely come.

Before I turn to a more detailed consideration of the shadow side of the unconscious, let me try to describe the essence of that concept by using a modern piece of equipment as an analogy. Remember that all analogies have their limitations and should not be pressed beyond these, it may be helpful to say that the unconscious, in a very real sense, is like the cassette tape. It records everything that happens to us. From the moment that we come into the world, every experience 'goes on tape'. Some would argue—and I am not at all disposed to disagree with them—that that tape begins to run before birth. Pre-natal experience of an unhappy kind may then play a part in life's later problems.[4]

It is that tape that has on it the hidden memories that may need to be healed, memories which, if not dealt with, may fester and ferment to our discomfort and pain. What is so crucial is that these memories are beyond our reach. However far we can remember early experience, it is not usual to be able to go back as far as our first two years of life, and certainly not to the critically important first year.

Yet these years are, in development terms, very important years. If we have been blessed by enjoying love and security in the years in which our personality is being formed, the chances of our being mature and generally happy adults are the greater. If we were unwanted children, or the wrong gender and so a disappointment, or objects of attempted abortion, and so on, then we have felt severe rejection and that recorded hurt may well follow us, if we do not come to terms with it in a positive way (or in the jargon 'work through it'). We may develop a sense not only of 'unwanted-ness', but a conviction that we lack worth, lack talent and lack acceptability. The possibilities of making lasting or deep relationships will certainly be diminished thereby.

There are many who have been so damaged in the client lists of counselling centres. If your parents have tried to destroy you before you were born, it says little for the value which they put on you. To be unwanted is to be rejected and the pain of rejection from unremembered but real experiences is very great.

If I could take the analogy of the tape-recorder a little further, we can see how, when we re-run the tape, that which is recorded on it lives again for us. The tape of life can be rewound and the experiences on it brought to life again. We do this deliberately with the real recorder. With the tape of our lives, the process often happens involuntarily. We find ourselves in some situation or in the presence of someone who activates a hidden memory. A great deal of the unhappy experience is felt again and we will find ourselves to be very uncomfortable as a result. Fear, anxiety, insecurity, rejection—all these feelings may arise, but because the original experience is beyond our reach in memory terms, we do not know why that particular situation is making us so tense or that person's presence, although we have never seen him/her before, is proving so difficult.

The repetition of circumstances producing something of the original feeling is often compounded by our getting ourselves into situations which underline our first unhappy experience. The rejected girl needs a strong, protective husband who will give her security, but in the end his gifts and talents are so marked over against hers that her lack of a sense of worth is actually re-emphasised, and the unhappy feelings increase. If a family arrives, and they too are gifted, then further attention is drawn to that sense of uselessness and misery is worse compounded. The rejected person so easily lands in situations that seem to be helpful and good, but in the end increase the inner damage.

People who have that kind of disturbing effect on us are probably unlucky in attracting to themselves such hostility and aggression from those they have never seen before. What is happening is that something about them—whether it be mannerism, voice, style—is 'flicking the switch' and is triggering off the memory (again, unconscious) of someone we have known or by whom we have been adversely affected, who provided a very unhappy experience for us. We are 'projecting' on to the one who is present, without any valid objective reasons, negative feelings which belong somewhere else.

If this concept of the unconscious is accepted, it will show us very clearly how our early hidden experiences, beyond normal recall, play such a part in our mid-life experience. That it is not our fault that we were so badly treated, while a matter for hurt and regret, is in one way irrelevant. We must take responsibility for who we are. The problems arising from the failure of others towards us may be, or feel, unfair, but they are *our* problems. They are part of us. We must accept our responsibility for them and act accordingly. There is no point in going through life constantly blaming others for our dis-ease. We must get on with trying to understand our problems and find the healing we need for them, whatever the method.[5]

What, however, is the relationship of these hidden, unhealed memories to health? To answer this, let us go back to the heart of the matter and that is the view of modern holistic medicine and the ancient biblical view of man as a physical, mental, emotional and spiritual being ('heart, soul, mind and strength' as, once again, the great commandment puts it).[6] If there is the interdependence of which I have written between these aspects of our being, that same principle holds true in the unconscious places and indeed even more so. Negative, unhappy memories, unhealed, festering in the inner being, may well translate themelves into bodily illnesses.

We do not get rid of such memories by pretending they do not exist, or that they are not on the tape. Suppressed feelings are not feelings of which we have rid ourselves. They are feelings that are denied and that, though banished to the unconscious, are real and active. They 'will out'. Psychosomatic illness, whether of body, heart or soul, may result in, indeed, dis-ease in the whole being.

I will try to set out briefly the ways in which the memories can be healed later, but first I must say a little more about this 'shadow', as the way we deal with our unacceptable selves is of crucial importance to our 'well-being'.

There are essentially four things to be said about the shadow. Before I set these down, it is important to realise—and especially important for those who are slightly or significantly critical of psychology—that in dealing with 'the shadow' I am not describing a purely psychological phenomenon which can only be discussed within that discipline. It is a spiritual phenomenon too. The fact is, however—and we must acknowledge it—that we are indebted to the great thinkers in the field of psychology for our better under-standing of this phenomenon—Freud and Jung and their successors. The phenomenon itself (the shadow side of the unconscious) is however dramatically set out in Romans 7:14–35. It is a passage to be read very slowly and deliberately, taking in the full import of what Paul is describing, for he is describing every one of us. Let me record it as it is presented first in the *Authorised Version* and then in the William Barclay translation which brings out the 'mystery of the unconscious'.[7] I have italicised statements that particularly point to the spiritual dilemma.

14   For we know that the law is spiritual: but I am carnal, sold under sin.
15   *For that which I do I allow not: for what I would, that do I not; but what I hate, that I do.*
16   If then I do that which I would not, I consent unto the law that *it is* good.
17   Now then it is no more I that do it, but sin that dwelleth in me.

18   For I know that in me (that is, in my flesh,) dwelleth no good thing: *for to will is present with me; but how to perform that which is good I find not.*

19   *For the good that I would I do not: but the evil which I would not, that I do.*

20   Now if I do that I would not, it is no more I that do it, but sin that dwelleth in me.

21   *I find then a law, that, when I would do good, evil is present with me.*

22   *For I delight in the law of God after the inward man:*

23   *But I see another law in my members, warring against the law of my mind, and bringing me into captivity to the law of sin which is in my members.*

24   *O wretched man that I am! who shall deliver me from the body of this death?*

25   *I thank God through Jesus Christ our Lord.*

Romans 7:14–25a, *Authorised Version*

The William Barclay translation is as follows:

My own actions are a mystery to me. What I do is not what I want to do, but what I hate doing. The fact that I do not want to do what I do proves that I agree that the law is good. The fact is that it is not I who do it: it is sin which has its home in me. I am well aware that, as far as my lower nature goes, nothing good has its home in me. For the ability to wish to do the fine thing, I possess: the power to do it I do not possess. *It is not the good that I want to do that I actually do; it is the evil that I do not want to do that I keep on doing.* If I do what I do not want to do, it is no longer I who do it. It is the sin which has its home in me which does it. *I find it to be a principle of life that, even when I want to do the right thing, the one thing that I can do is the wrong thing. In my inner self I delight in the law of God but I am aware of a different law, operating in the physical parts of my body, and waging a constant campaign against the law which my reason accepts and reducing me to captivity to that sinful world which operates in my physical body.* I am a wretched creature. Who will rescue me from this body which turns life into death? God alone can—through Jesus Christ our Lord! Thanks be to him.

Romans 7:15–25a, *William Barclay translation*

This, you can see, is not just good contemporary psychology. It is profound religion. Psychology is a tool to be used as an aid to faith—for the more understanding we have of human nature the better, but it cannot be a substitute for faith, which too often it has become. The dilemma that Paul is describing and which is the fundamental problem for fallen humanity, is one that can only be dealt with *by grace*, the freely-given gift of God we can never deserve. It is for this reason that healing, wholeness and salvation need the solution which Paul proclaims. Wholeness and therefore health cannot be real and effective without the biblical doctrine of grace, a grace the Old Testament knew, the grace which became incarnate in Jesus Christ.

I return to my four statements about the shadow.

The *first* statement I make quite dogmatically, simply because it must be true. We all have a shadow side to our being. In religious language the texts are plainly written, 'All have sinned and fall short of the glory of God',[8] 'None is righteous, no, not one'.[9] Temptation is a common human factor. In psychological language, we would say that there are those inner pressures which come from the negative side of the unconscious and compel (or so it feels) us to 'act out' our needs. These pressures may be expressed in behaviour which is socially and/or ecclesiastically unacceptable.

Second, there comes the most ominous statement about the shadow side of the unconscious. Because of the inner pressures that may build up within us, for reasons which are a mystery to us, we are capable of very frightening attitudes, feelings and actions. We may go through life, year after year, occasionally having difficulty in containing these pressures and aware that, when our defences are down, or we are beyond the reach of the sanctions that may normally help us to 'keep control' or indeed when we are physically and/or nervously 'under par', we just cannot hold back the pressures that come from within us.

It is in this kind of situation that respected and honoured people can behave in such a way that they offend society and may reach the courts, or they may, additionally, offend church authorities and be deprived of their office.[10] Every single one of us ought to be careful of our readiness to judge or condemn people in such situations. It is *always* the case that we can and should say 'There but for the grace of God, go I'.

There are some areas of life and being in which we have to recognise the power of strong inner feelings breaking through the defences that contain them. It is my belief that violence is much nearer the surface of most of us than we would care to acknowledge. Yet we ought to recognise feelings of violence and acknowledge them when they are there for, unrecognised, they become dangerous. This is also true corporately. Living as we do in a violent society, the sources of violence must be examined. It may be that, apart from the sheer wickedness that much contemporary violence expresses, there are hidden frustrations and fears that, coming in a threatening way (authority, unemployment, the prospect of nuclear war, and so on) contribute to our present malaise.

The same anxiety is present in relation to racial prejudice. Clearly we are all against colour prejudice and at a conscious level, sincerely so. I suspect that at the unconscious level we are not nearly so confident about this. I have certainly myself observed situations in which it has been quite clear that group behaviour was deeply resented and likely to produce critical and indeed hostile reactions, where the offending group was coloured.[11] 'What right have they ... ?' hovers uneasily just below the level of consciousness and given stimulation, feelings can easily be aroused. We must never be casual in these areas. The shadow is real.

It is also right to re-emphasise here that there is a corporate aspect to the unconscious—Jung called it 'the collective unconscious'—and there is a collective shadow. The collective unconscious is formed by cultural and other influences which have shaped us. The fact, for example, that I was brought up in Scotland, in a manse and therefore church background, in a sabbatarian society, reinforced by parental attitudes to Sunday, and in a total abstinence culture, makes me different in my instinctive responses from someone born into a secular context in a rural English atmosphere, where cricket on the village green on a Sunday with a happy retreat to the local pub at the end of it is both normal and seen as healthy and good as well as socially acceptable. I am not concerned whether one way is wrong and the other right. I am simply concerned to demonstrate that I am a product of a set of social and/or religious circumstances and these will be reflected in my attitudes and especially in spontaneous responses when I am invited to engage in certain activities which are normal for my hosts or friends. (There is an important counselling point here. We must never assume that some situation which is normal for us is not a problem for someone else. It is a particularly important point in a multi-racial society.)

The 'collective shadow' is the corporate expression of negative attitudes and feelings. Nazi Germany must be the most obvious example of it, where a noble nation was caught up willy-nilly in doing the things it would not consciously want to do. A lot of crowd violence comes out of the same area. The reason I refer to this corporate aspect of behaviour is to stress the surprising and indeed frightening lengths to which the shadow—individually and corporately—can push us.

The *third* statement about the shadow—and this is important for both health and healing—is the need to accept that dark side of our nature. It is only in the acceptance of the shadow that hope lies.

I regard this point as of the greatest possible importance for I have no doubt that the road to wholeness is determined by our ability to come to positive terms with the shadow side of our being. 'You shall love the Lord your God with all your heart, and with all your soul, and with all your mind and with all your strength and ... your neighbour as yourself' says the greatest of all commandments (Mark 12:30–31). It is only as we are able to love ourselves—that is accept and love our unacceptable and unloveable selves—that we will be able truly to love our neighbour with his/her unacceptable self. If Christian pastoral care is, in fact, the acceptance of people where they are in order to (and this is important) take them to where God wants them to be, then it does imply the acceptance of others, 'warts and all'. The capacity to do that resides in our ability humbly to accept ourselves, 'warts and all'.

That this is right and proper is based, of course, on the solid fact that God accepts us 'warts and all' (Oliver Cromwell, 1599–1658). He is not interested only in the more pleasant aspects we present. He is concerned with us as we are, people made in his image, people who are victims of a corrupt and fallen society, people who share the common factor of a sinful or negative aspect to our nature. The whole thrust of pastoral care lies in the acceptance and love by God of his people which is in itself the motivation for the accepting of others in love.

It is, then, a primary duty for us all to ensure that we take ourselves to the desert place,[12] be it a barren place such as those in which John and Paul spent long periods or, as it must usually be for most of us, the corner of a room which is 'our sanctuary', our 'desert place'. This is the place where we have to come face to face with God and face to face with ourselves. The God who makes his 'absolute demand' on us in the same breath promises his 'final succour'.[13]

The call to the Christian to be self-aware and to face up to all the implications of that personal encounter with God is a primary condition of spiritual growth and progress in sanctification. It is in this way that we grow into Christ. It is the way to that health and wholeness we so earnestly seek. The denial of that dark side, with a refusal to look at ourselves in honesty and frankness, is both pointless and dangerous. Evil is never overcome by pretending it does not exist. The devil becomes much more determined and subtle when he senses such an attitude. Evil is only dealt with by confrontation and acceptance. The Cross was primarily that meeting of good and evil in conflict. The victory was the Lord's.

That same victory is promised to those who are willing to see themelves as they are and commit the whole matter in trust to God. To be ready and willing to face ourselves as God sees us is to set our feet on the road to victory.

The *fourth* statement is one of hope and vision. It is that, as I believe, the surrendering of our unacceptable self to God's redemptive love may issue in the greatest blessing of all, that it is that bit of ourselves we found it hard to face that God will find potentially creative. It may well be that the part we felt we had to hold back is the very part that, once redeemed, he can most fruitfully use.

I have developed this point in other places,[14] but I cannot go on further without trying as I did then to explain the intuition—for intuition rather than reason proffers this view—that sees great hope in our giving to God that dark side of our being. It may be that Paul himself is evidence of it. A man whose personality was marked by a very aggressive trait (persecuting the Christians, breathing out threatenings and slaughter against Christian disciples,[15] approving of Stephen's death,[16]) found that same aggressive power had come to be the servant of the Lord as a result of his encounter with Jesus on the Damascus Road. Paul had the same personality structure as before but now the dominant characteristic of it—sheer aggressive force—which had so far been used so destructively had now become the very energy that took him on his staggering missionary journeys; that enabled him to cope courageously with all he had to face as the 'least of the apostles'.

It is worth looking for examples of this principle in other places. I, for example, see it as applying in that narrow area between lust and love.

I had, some years ago, to write a small book about Colonel Alida Bosshardt, the Dutch Salvation Army officer known throughout Holland and indeed far beyond that country.[17] Colonel Bosshardt has spent nearly 30 years in ministry in the Red Light district of Amsterdam. She saw her ministry there, not as getting rid of the area—that, because of human demand, was impossible—but of serving within it those caught up in prostitution. She knew virtually every girl in that district — over 2000 of them. She was accepted and loved by every section of that community whatever their trade or profession.

I recall Colonel Bosshardt saying on one occasion that she sometimes felt that she was 'a kind of Christian prostitute'. In that puzzling statement, I 'heard' her saying that had the Lord not called her to his service, she could easily have been on the other side of that line between destructive lust and creative love.

The need to love and be loved is very much part of the motivation—always mixed—that takes us into our life's calling to be a pastor, in whatever form it is expressed. It is to be where love can be given creatively and love can be graciously received. It was the desire to love and be loved that, had it been unredeemed, could perhaps have led her to the same Red Light area in another rôle. Under God, she was enabled to offer amazingly loving service to multitudes in need.

The thought is an intriguing and a creative one. I believe that it may well have been borne out in the lives of many people. And where that miracle of grace has happened, there is a health-promoting factor at work that will lead in the direction of wholeness.

It is therefore an individual Christian responsibility to be as in touch as we can be with the unconscious side of our being; to be as aware as we possibly can be of our hidden self is essential generally but particularly so if we are involved in any kind of intimate therapeutic relationship. In the *general* context, I make this point, because, for the spiritual life of any of us, it is essential to acknowledge our sinfulness, failure, weakness, the potential there is in our dark side to do hurt, damage, wrong—whatever term we prefer to use in this context. It is a consequence of that acknowledgement that we may well see the wonder of God's forgiveness, the magnanimity of God's grace and the infinity of God's love. It is the experience of those who travel the way of sanctification that our growth in grace only makes more clear the extent of our rebellion. The saint who is furthest along the road that leads to life is the one who will totally acknowledge the sinful state by which we are afflicted. And in all confession, it is not just sins that need to be acknowledged but sin itself.

We also need to develop self-awareness in the particular context of pastoral care. In intimate therapeutic relationship, there are psychological mechanisms that can easily get to work. Such mechanisms operate at the unconscious level. In the language of psychology, they include what is known as 'transference' and 'counter-transference'. These mechanisms can develop strength when the person to whom we are ministering begins to see us in a different rôle. We may, in terms of the relationship, come to be seen as some important figure in their lives, for example, father, mother, lover, and they relate to us not as ourselves but in those rôles. So feelings belonging to that other important relationship are transferred to us. There are implications in this process so we need to be aware of what is happening in the relationship. 'Counter-transference' is the same process the other way round, that is the counsellor is now seeing the person seeking help as a daughter, son and so on. What would be appropriate to such a relationship is likely not to be appropriate to a therapist-client or a 'helper/helped' relationship. In other words, if we are not to some extent aware of the kind of things which, very subtly, happen at the unconscious level, we may end up in a relationship of great difficulty.

How can we become more self-aware and be in touch with our deeper feelings?

First, there is the opportunity a therapeutic relationship for oneself provides, to look at the problems arising in relationships with others. It is for this reason that most responsible and recognised counselling training programmes either insist or strongly recommend that their trainees are themselves in such a relationship. This is called 'personal therapy'. It is the place in which one can not only discuss and share such problems but test out feelings in a safe and secure context—which is one of the prime functions of therapy. Outside such a context, such complications could break up the relationship. In the therapeutic context, things that go wrong in the relationship are not damaging to it. Nothing that happens destroys the relationship. Next week, at the same time, in the same place, the relationship will be intact and ready to continue.

Clearly the deeper the level of therapeutic relationship, the heavier the demand is for training in self-awareness. For that reason counselling may properly expect personal therapy once a week, psychotherapeutic training two or three times a week, and training to be an analyst four or five times a week.

These deeper technical areas lie outside the immediate context of our discussion of self-awareness, but the practices I have referred to indicate the importance given in professional circles to self-awareness and the understanding of the unconscious.

Second, dreams are important for getting into touch with the unconscious. This is a large subject which again lies outside the scope of this book, but it may be helpful to indicate this source of self-knowledge. When we sleep, the conscious part of our being is put to rest, but the unconscious neither slumbers nor sleeps. Indeed it is the more active in those circumstances. Messages will come from the unconscious through dreams but they may be too threatening for us to hear and so they are expressed in complicated symbols and symbolism—to help disguise them. It is certainly wise to give attention to the content of our dreams. There are often highly informative clues to where we are and perhaps where we ought to be.

The 'Freudian slip' is sometimes an amusing, and on occasion a devastating, insight into what we really feel at the unconscious level. It is that slip we make when we use a word or phrase we did not mean to use but which expresses a real feeling when courtesies do not allow such frankness. The study of our Freudian slips may tell us quite a lot!

There are in this field, especially nowadays, many quaint and curious therapies on offer, just as the so-called 'alternative' field is full of, at best, unusual and, at worst, bizarre approaches to healing. The whole field, whether 'psychotherapeutic' or 'healing', is one in which the age-old command to 'test the spirits' holds good.[18] As a general rule it is sensible to stay with those methods or disciplines that have authentic training programmes and recognisable structures, and to be wary of teachers whose whole training is no more than a few sessions or a crash weekend. It is the lack of standards in so many of (as I would prefer to call them) the complementary therapies that prevents orthodox medicine, operating on very high and sophisticated standards, from recognising or taking seriously many such approaches. We dare not close the door to new knowledge, for God has endless gifts to offer, but we do need to be sensible and careful when we are seeking help for our inner being and all that implies. Too often the Humpty-Dumpty Syndrome is present in the less responsible, unrecognised techniques of the alternative field. There are many so-called therapists who can take us apart and to bits, but they cannot always put us together again—we are left to pick up the pieces.

That cautionary word given, I end this chapter with a strong plea for recognition of the need to know ourselves, as we are. There is always hope where there is a willingness to face the pain of growth, be it in the counselling room or, in the spiritual context, in the desert place.

Notes to Chapter 9

1 The 'shadow' is the Jungian term for the negative side of the unconscious.

2 Psalm 42:7

3 Romans 8:16

4 Work I was involved in with someone who had not completed primal therapy with Dr Frank Lake by the time he died, gave me insight into this kind of therapeutic process.

5 Whether psychotherapy or 'prayer healing' and so on.

6 See chapter 3.

7 I have used the two versions to try to bring home the importance of this statement.

8 Romans 3:23

9 Romans 3:10

10 There are specific cases where this has happened, but I prefer not to bring them to mind and thus continue the grief and unhappiness of those involved. The way a well-known politician is repeatedly quoted, thus bringing back his pain, is to be condemned. He has devoted a great deal of his life to good works— which only makes media unwillingness to forget his failures open to censure.

11 I am thinking of tube train situations in which there has been rush-hour jostling. The reactions seem to be notably more hostile if the offenders happen to be coloured.

12 I have used 'the desert place' as the literal or metaphorical place of encounter with God in my book, *Creative Silence* (Arthur James, 1980).

13 H H Farmer, *The World and God*

14 See note 12 above. See also my book *Love, the Word that heals* (Arthur James, 1981).

15 Acts 9:1

16 Acts 8:1 and 22:20. The *Authorised Version* uses the word 'consenting', but William Barclay uses the stronger word 'approving'.

17 Denis Duncan, *Here is my Hand* (Hodder & Stoughton, 1977). Now out of print.

18 'Try the spirits whether they are of God', I John 4:1, *Authorised Version*. William Barclay uses the word 'test'.

10

The Healing of the Memories

'The Healing of the Memories' is a phrase that has been used a good deal in the healing field in recent years, and particularly by those drawn to evangelical emphases that stress the need to take Jesus, the authority, at his word. The concept is also in line with what I have written in the chapter on *The Unconscious*, but is expressed there in more psychological terms and dealt with in a different way in the psychotherapeutic approach.

Let me begin with the healing world.

I have set out already something of the methods of the counselling and psychotherapeutic disciplines to hidden memories. Here I use the word counselling in the specific sense in which it is represented by mainstream counselling approaches.[1] The essence of the method is the belief that if we can discover and face the things which are getting in the way of our proper growth and deal with them by acknowledging these obstacles and integrating them into our whole personality, then we shall have made some progress on the road to maturity, or individuation, or wholeness.[2] What we do not know threatens us. What we do know we can try to face. To become aware of our 'hang-ups' or 'blocks' is the first big step in dealing with them.

The process, as it is represented in mainstream counselling today, is practised, as I have established, without reference to a specifically and explicitly Christian model. Most of the work is effected by 'psychological/spiritual' (with a small 's') means. The mainstream counselling agencies in this country, like the American disciplines from which they have emerged, have a foundation which is manifestly spiritual but is not necessarily specifically Christian.

I do not feel it would be helpful to introduce here a discussion

on what *'Christian* Counselling' is. I have referred already—
but only in passing—to the models in which the Christian
vocabulary and means of grace are acknowledged and used
as against the approach of (as I define it) mainstream counselling. This is based on a recognition of the spiritual dimension,
but quite deliberately does not equate 'spiritual' with 'Christian'.
Counsellors who are Christians claim they take themselves
into the counselling room, and so are involved in 'Christian
counselling'. The Christian element is in their own faith and
the attitudes it implies, and that which makes them what they
are. They might never use specifically Christian language—
unless of course the client introduced the material—and they
would not feel they wanted to engage in explicitly religious
references or suggest, for example, prayer. The process
followed would then not be dissimilar to work done by a
counsellor who recognised the spiritual dimension but was
not Christian.

There is no doubt that there is a wide gap in approach
between counsellors trained in that discipline and those
engaged in the healing of the memories from an evangelical
or charismatic standpoint. It would be, for example, normal
for the latter to speak of the presence and power of the Holy
Spirit in such healing, to engage in prayer and to give the
'credit' entirely to that 'divine activity'.[3] A counsellor in the
psychotherapeutic/analytic tradition, if a Christian, would
feel that the Holy Spirit was very much 'the third person' in
the room, but would see that power much more as that which
enables the client to work through their problems for themselves because only if they themselves make the changes
needed can change occur. The difference is in a sense that
between the Holy Spirit in the evangelical/charismatic view
doing something *to* the client as a result of which he or she is
different or changed, and in the analytic tradition the client
working through difficulties by seeking to understand them
and face them, and in the light of that insight making changes
in the pattern of their lives. In this case, for the Christian who
is a counsellor working on the psychotherapeutic model, the
Spirit would be the resource that provided the strength to
make the changes, but not the one that does it for us. It is with
the Spirit's help, that the pain of growth can be faced.

There is then a wide gap in approach and technique between what I am calling mainstream counselling and, for example, the Jay Adams model of counselling which is bible-centred, Spirit-orientated and very explicitly Christian. There is, as I have tried to show, a similar sort of gap between 'counselling' (representing one discipline) and 'healing' which has a different basis.

I do not want to make too much of the issue. It is my impression that the gap between healing and counselling, using these words to describe the two approaches, is closing a little. There are some counselling centres which insist on all their staff being Christian and church-committed, and which offer both healing and counselling, and which have a chapel within the centre.[4] But they are few.

The other approach to the healing of the memories, or as that greatly honoured pioneer of healing, Agnes Sanford,[5] called it 'healing of the emotions', is much more focussed on praying the person in need back to the hidden memories, staying with them when they have reached that painful point, and then using techniques like visualisation to bring peace. To see the Lord present in your situation, dwell on how he would see the problem and respond to it, and feel his answer to it, will ease the pain. There are agencies which devote the whole of their time and energy to ministry of this kind and claim extensive results and healings through it.

As in so many other fields of work, it is important to minister in the way one's own temperament determines. There are those who would simply not feel at home in prayer counselling—that would, I expect, refer to probably all of those in analytically orientated disciplines. There are those with a particular kind of zealous faith who would find it impossible to work within the limits and boundaries of the psychotherapeutic model. What is important is that people minister through their own temperaments and do things in the way that feels comfortable to them.

There is, then, a range of models of counselling and all have value in their own way. It is desirable that people work within the approach that represents where they are, rather than force their ministries inside a model that is restricting. That would limit the Spirit's work for them.

The ultimate need is that we keep in sight the aim and purpose of whatever ministry we adopt. Some would express that as 'deliverance';[6] some as bringing people to Christ; some as helping people to find wholeness; some as enabling growth in personality and that maturity which is the goal of sound emotional development.

Others would see the hurtful memories as the work of Satan from which deliverance is the only hope. Some would regard unhealed memories as blocks to be identified and worked through. Some would prefer the concept of healing energies flowing through the nervous system, a process based on energy systems coming from Eastern understandings of the way energies, positive and negative, flow through our being.

There is, in my experience, a great deal of intolerance in the fields I have just been discussing. For many in the healing ministry field, any approach which does not show itself to be wholly 'Christ-centred' cannot be tolerated at all.[7] I find that level of intolerance essentially inconsistent with the spirit of Christianity and indeed with the 'flexibility round the edges' to which I have already referred as typical of Jesus but not necessarily the disciples. The aforementioned incident in which the disciples complained to Jesus that there was someone healing in his name but who was not one of them seems to show that the disciples expected Jesus to march over to the offender, rebuke him and ask him to cease his activity. In fact, as we saw, Jesus did not do so. Rather, he expressed a degree of tolerance which the disciples had not expected. 'Forbid him not, for he that is not against us is for us' (Luke 9:50 AV).

Let me make my own position crystal clear. I believe that the only healer is Christ, the risen and ascended Lord and that it is only on that basis and in that name that I can work and minister. I have all through this book maintained that the redemptive gift—which is given in Jesus—is essential to wholeness and that without the miracle of grace, we cannot be made whole. That is as I see it, and I can see it in no other way. I shall therefore always proclaim that as my understanding of the healing way. It is a Christ-centred approach and the longer I go on in ministry, the more I believe it to be the right stance—for me. But I would rather proclaim that stance as my witness to the truth than feel it necessary to condemn utterly those who do not take that same precise view. For there are diversities of gifts and the Spirit is behind them all.[8]

I have no right to try to confine God to one way which happens to be my own. I certainly have no right to put ecclesiastical boundaries round the Spirit and proclaim that he cannot operate in any other place or way. I am as jealous for the Lord as others—some might say too jealous—but as I only see through a glass darkly, I cannot dogmatically lay it down that the divine activity that is the Spirit is not expressed in ways I have not seen or do not understand. God must be free to be active in whatever way he wills. I do not think I serve the Lord best by condemning out of hand those who also minister in his name and through his power and to his glory, but happen to embrace a particular approach which I cannot justify. I must be convinced and definite in *my* positive witness. I do not thereby have the right to decry the ministries, and the integrity, of others.

In the ministry to the healing of the memories, there is room for varied approaches to the hidden hurts and un-happy, unremembered experiences that create dis-ease and ultimately disease. There are many sincere groups and individuals deeply involved in prayer counselling and personal prayer ministries. There are many who approach such heal-ing through the psychotherapeutic discipline. In both spheres, many are helped. What I do ask is that neither group makes wild and generalised claims that have little or no substance. Both groups will say—and do say, as does every agency in the healing and counselling field—that they have too often to pick up the pieces after what they see as a mishandling of human problems! That points really not to insincerity, but to limited knowledge. From whatever point of view we minister, we see only a part, so error and failure, as the disciples found too, are unavoidable. What is needed is a much greater deter-mination to try to create some sort of mutual understanding of the way others minister in Christ's name and to bring about the integration of healing and counselling as the full expression of the healing ministry in our time.

The roots of the separation as I have said go deep into theology but, in the end, there must be a coming together of the approaches that are each based on an over-emphasis of one element in our experience of God as immanent and transcendent. I see the process presently at work as integration through the Spirit.

There is however one key element in whatever approach we may make to the healing of the memories and to that, as I believe, the most important doctrine of all for health and healing, I now turn, but first a word about co-operation.

Notes to Chapter 10

1   By 'mainstream counselling approaches' I refer to the model most counselling centres in the Association of Pastoral Care and Counselling division of the British Association for Counselling use.
2   'Individuation' is C G Jung's word. 'Wholeness' in this book refers to the Christian understanding of healing and health, that ideal which is God's will for us.
3   The London Healing Mission is an example of this method.
4   The St Barnabas Ecumenical Centre for Christian Healing and Counselling is one of the best known examples of the effort to hold these two words together. As Chairman of it for some seven years, I know the splendid way that Centre serves and the very significant quality of its leaders and staff. A Eucharist is held weekly in the St Barnabas chapel and healing services take place there. It is in Derby Street, Norwich.
5   Two of Agnes Sanford's books are still in print—*The Healing Light* and *Healing Gifts of the Spirit* (Arthur James).
6   For a useful book on deliverance and exorcism, see *Deliverance* edited by Michael Perry (SPCK, 1987).
7   This is very much in evidence in attitudes to the field of complementary medicine.
8   I Corinthians 12:4

11

Forgiveness

We play a part in the creation of our illnesses so we must play a part in the restoration of health.

That statement is an important one for the ministry of healing. It is another way of saying that healing is not so much God doing something *to* us, but rather doing something *with* us and *through* us. In other words, there is a divine-human co-operation in healing. We play a part in our healing.

The principle of co-operation runs through the whole range of our relationship to God as the Bible presents it. 'We are labourers together with God' Paul says[1]—or fellow-workers with him as one of the translations renders it.[2] God is the 'principal'—without him we can do nothing, but we have a part to play.[3] It is a subordinate part, but at the same time it is an essential part.

This principle of co-operation is expressed in prayer. It is God who acts but we have to ask, seek, knock.[4]

Intercession is a meaningless undertaking if our part in it is without point or value. What the New Testament presents to us is the picture—especially in the story of the importunate widow[5]—of our part in prayer as an essential contribution. In a way that it is impossible to understand, we play a part in bringing about change, for change for the better is the point of intercession. Prayer is an exercise in divine-human co-operation.

It is the same in the Sacraments. As I have already indicated, there is no efficacy in a sacrament if there is no faith.[6] Faith is the human contribution without which there cannot be a sacrament.

Let us apply this principle of co-operation to our healing. If we have damaged our lungs through too much smoking or our kidneys through too much alcohol, we have a right to come to the altar-rail and ask for healing. If, however, we rise from that rail and go back to our cigarettes or our glass, we cannot be healed, not because God does not want to heal us, but because we are not, in proper co-operation, playing our part.

If we are damaging ourselves by over-eating, we have every right to pray for our healing from over-weight or indigestion, but we must not get up from the rail and go and gorge ourselves again. No, there is a part *we* have to play in order to co-operate with God's desire that we should be more whole. And a painful part it is. We have to understand why we over-eat and, of course, find that over-eating is not what we do to satisfy our physical hunger. It is what we do to satisfy our *emotional* hunger and emotional needs. To work on that problem and through it will indeed demand effort on our part.

(There is, incidentally, another situation in which we over-eat and ironically it is brought about by our training in a good principle! If we were taught to live by the rule 'waste not, want not', the sight of left-over buns or cakes may distress us, but the solution we choose to avoid such waste is to clear the plate! It becomes a complicated moral and emotional problem!)

I want to take the examples I have used so far, one step further. If we feel a bitter resentment in our heart, for example towards a dead parent, or an inability to forgive someone and be reconciled, we may take our concern over such feelings to the altar-rail and ask to be relieved of them. There will however be, in any release we are given, an obligation to follow through that release and deal with the problem of our resentment. Our healing is again a continuation of the action of the healing God plus our own effort to put right any wrong situation for which we may be responsible in whole or in part.

'Do you want to be healed?' (John 5:6). This was the question Jesus put to the impotent man. We can say 'no' to that question—albeit unconsciously—for we may not want to let the benefits of illness go. But if we do withhold our co-operation we cannot be truly healed. God does not heal us against our will. He works with us, that is in co-operation with us to help us to be whole.

The theme of forgiveness raised in the third example brings us to the Christian doctrine which I believe to be of most importance for the healing ministry. It is the doctrine of forgiveness.

Deep in the human heart is the need to be reconciled both to God and to others. We live uneasily with feelings of separation and isolation. The absence of forgiveness and reconciliation creates inner turmoil and those hearts that are restless will be so until they rest comfortably with God.

Such unease can express itself in guilt. Now, guilt is a proper and appropriate feeling. If we have done wrong, we should feel guilty. The absence of a sense of guilt from situations where it ought to be felt is a bigger worry than its presence. There is however a difference between guilt which is appropriate and guilt which is not. That inappropriate guilt is a worry because it is a guilt which persists beyond the point where it is necessary. It becomes an all-embracing feeling, unrelated to particular events about which we ought to *feel* guilty until they are, in the language of scripture, 'taken away'. Once sins are confessed and forgiven, we may rightly grieve over the circumstances that made us guilty, but the power of those situations to hurt us or destroy us no longer exists. So we experience the glory of forgiveness, the greatest blessing our faith has to offer.

The answer to guilt is truly forgiveness. We must not, however, assume that in the reality of life it is as easy as that. It is possible to believe at the rational level, in the doctrine of forgiveness and to know, intellectually, that God forgives 'till seventy times seven',[7] but it is quite another matter to feel forgiven. It is on this rock there is so much stumbling, for we constantly meet, in pastoral situations, the chronically guilty whose inability to feel forgiven is, literally, making them ill.

The sad aspect of this particular form of distress—and it is an aspect that, in ministry to such people, we must remember—is that however often we declare in words the Gospel of forgiveness to be true and universal, those words simply have no effect. People want to believe what we say and, at the mental level, do, but they still cannot experience it. Unfortunately it is very difficult to know the truth of that which we have not experienced.

The problems arising from inappropriate, or, as it can become, pathological guilt are complicated. If such guilt remains undealt with, it may extend from particular problems—often peccadilloes rather than sins—to the whole of life itself. It is then that we find ourselves faced with that sad and troubled soul who is guilty simply because he/she is alive.

It is in this kind of area that I feel anxious about the ministry of the enthusiastic amateur (although the root of the word amateur, is from the Latin verb *amare* meaning to 'love') and the danger of over-simplification. In psychotherapeutic terms, there is a great deal of technical, professional work to be done in such sad situations. On the other hand we must never deny the possibility of the divine power breaking through in such situations. I would deny the faith I have if I did not believe in divine surprises. Whatever the answer to such guilt is, however, our only real hope is the Christian teaching on forgiveness.

How can people be brought back to health if they cannot feel that they are forgiven? How can people be made to feel the forgiveness to which the Bible testifies?

Prayer for them will help, for prayer is power. Prayer with them will take them along the road to healing. In the end, they are however most likely to experience forgiveness when they meet it in a person. This underlines the importance of 'healing relationship'. God ministers to our healing through people.

Once again it is clear that the healing ministry begins with any one of us and involves every one who claims to be a Christian. The Christian is, by definition, committed to healing relationship.

The problem of guilt is a particular one and an exceedingly difficult one. In cases where guilt has become inappropriate, specialist help is usually needed. My concern here is to stress the healing power of forgiveness and the health that comes from being forgiven—by God certainly, and by others too. To be restored to a right relationship with God is, in one sense, the ultimate healing. To have our relationships with others restored through mutual forgiveness and love is health-giving indeed.

Wholeness can be helpfully defined in terms of relationship.

When, as I said earlier, we are in a right relationship with God (upwards), with the earth (downwards), with our neighbours (outwards) and with ourselves (inwards), we are indeed on the way to true health. It is a basic task of the Christian healing ministry to do all it can to enable these fundamental relationships to be fully in operation. It is of the essence of the life and work of the healing community to make it possible for all our relationships to be in good order. It is indeed here that one of the corporate aspects of healing ministry applies.

It is not possible for me to say how, outside the Christian doctrine of forgiveness, that real peace of mind can come. It is not for me either to say that such cannot be. I simply testify that the glory of the Christian faith is, in my experience, its doctrine of forgiveness and that that teaching is one of the greatest contributions to our healing that I know. Forgiveness and healing dwell together.

If forgiveness is so powerful a healing agency, the value of the practice of confession in some form is thereby underlined, and the healing community must make provision for it. The older forms of confession have lost their place in churches traditionally committed to the practice, but the 'sacrament of consultation' which must include that opportunity, is slowly taking its place. Whatever the traditions of the denomination to which we happen to belong, the value of confession as a step on the road to healing simply has to be acknowledged. Confession is indeed good for the soul. The ultimate importance of the practice of confession is that it opens the door to forgiveness, and forgiveness brings with it the promise of renewal, new vision, new life. This, I say again, is the healing way.

The healing community, if it is to be true to that description, must always be a loving, forgiving, accepting, encouraging and renewing body. How can the body of Christ stand back from a total commitment to the healing ministry when its whole *raison d'etre* is to make men and women whole?

Notes to Chapter 11

1   I Corinthians 3:9, *Authorised Version*
2   *New English Bible*, *New International Version* and *Revised Standard Version*
3   For example, see John 3:27 or Psalm 127:1.
4   Matthew 7:7
5   Luke 18:1–8
6   See chapter 8 page 87.
7   I remember J B Phillips, when in the midst of that depression that lasted a decade—about which he has written publicly (Denis Duncan, Editor, *Through the Year with J B Phillips*, Arthur James) telling me he had lost all feeling as a result of 'the dark night of the soul'. He could no longer feel any emotion or indeed enjoy music which he formerly loved so much.

12

The Healing Ministry—Some Questions

It is not possible within the short compass of a book such as this to deal with all the questions that arise over the ministry of healing. In that there has been recently published a book that makes it its whole purpose to answer as many as possible of these practical questions, it is sufficient to refer readers to that title. It is *Healing Is Wholeness* and is described as 'A Resource Book to encourage Healing Ministry initiatives in the Local Church'. The author is Howard Booth who is the Adviser on Health and Healing Ministries to the Division of Social Responsibility of the Methodist Church and Vice-Chairman of The Churches' Council for Health and Healing. The book carries the imprimatur of both the Methodist Division of Social Responsibility and The Churches' Council for Health and Healing.[1]

Healing Is Wholeness devotes the whole of its first chapter to questions about healing services, chapter 2 to 'Praying for Healing' and chapter 3 to 'Healing and Evangelism'. Chapter 4 provides seven Bible studies on healing, and chapter 5 seven magazine or newsletter articles. Chapter 6 offers sample orders of service. There are appendices on resources of various kinds. Obviously from what I have said, this is a thoroughly practical book related to the working out of the concepts I have tried to discuss here. The only way in which I propose to duplicate this is by including, as an Appendix, some indication about resources of various kinds available in this field.[2]

I confine myself in this chapter to making a brief comment on one or two matters in some way associated with health and healing that could benefit from further comment.

A Place To Begin

How do we begin to develop the healing ministry in our parish situation or local church? The question has been answered very specifically in the video *The Healing Ministry*, already mentioned.[3] The Revd John Schild, vicar of a church in the Potters Bar area just outside London, tells of the steps taken there to initiate such a ministry. The essential elements in it were (a) a long period of preparation; (b) a great deal of teaching; (c) a careful consideration of the whole question by the Parochial Church Council; and (d) actually beginning services of blessing by the laying on of hands. The ministry has continued and developed in that parish, and 'we have never regretted taking that step' says John Schild.

In my own involvement in setting up such a ministry, the pattern was along similar lines. The initial step was to create a group whose weekly purpose was to intercede, by name, for people in need. The next step was the provision of a Bible study group where reflection on matters of the faith could take place. This followed a series of Lenten meetings on healing ministry. It was from those bases that it seemed right to suggest *to the church as a whole* that a ministry of healing service should be held regularly (once a month was the initial frequency) and that blessing by laying on of hands should take place there. This is always preceded by teaching on the healing ministry so that all are as aware as possible of what the focus of the service is—that the power of the risen Christ should be channelled through the church, the healing community, to make those who receive the ministry more whole.

I italicised the phrase 'to the church as a whole' to stress the importance of the whole church being part of the agreement to move in this direction. The ministry must not be a fringe activity, but must be a part of the church's total witness. Not everyone may agree with the decision to move forward in this way, but the step will be taken only after the church as a whole (however that is expressed in the different policies of the denominations) has considered the matter and made a policy decision about it. The ministry should not be forced into the life of a congregation.

As the ministry is given to the whole church, lay people who have experience of it can take part in the laying on of hands. Ministry can be by one person, or two working together. It is important that there should not be any sense of rush or haste for, in that moment when hands are laid, God's love is focussed on that one person—and all present are involved in the act through prayer.

With large congregations, a lot of time is needed to give ministry in the right kind of way, so enough people should be available for ministry to make the service of suitable length.

It is important both for those so involved, and also as a demonstration of an important principle, that ministrants should minister to each other before offering ministry themselves. The principle being visibly demonstrated in this way is that we are *all* in need of health, healing and wholeness.

The relationship between healing and counselling, however that word is interpreted, is important. There is one sense in which there ought always to be counselling support available after a service, but it is not possible for every church which has such a service to set up such an ideal situation. What should not happen—although it sometimes does—is the turning of the *liturgical* occasion into a counselling session. It is not appropriate to have counselling sessions at the altar rail. Wherever these sessions take place, they must, for obvious and practical reasons, be outside the act of worship.

It may be of help to both those ministering and those to whom ministry is being given for the latter to give their first name, if it is not already known, to express in a whispered word any particular need or situation and to ask for prayer and blessing for another in need.

The words used by the ministrant need not be in the same form each time, nor used identically by all ministrants, but it is helpful if there is a common part to it that is always or at least invariably included. That said, it is wise to leave space for the Spirit to guide us all to minister in a particular way. Both order and flexibility are therefore important indicators in this matter.

The decision as to whether laying on of hands should always be within a Eucharistic context is largely a local one. The Eucharist is manifestly a healing Sacrament—indeed it is so above all others. Some therefore feel it is the right context for the additional blessing by the laying on of hands, and there is little to be said against that—although the sheer practicalities of such a service can be difficult. If it is allowed at all (as I think it should be) to think of worship in 'theatrical' terms, it may be that the need to focus on two high points in worship so close together reduces the effect of each element. The ultimate decision is a local one and the discussion of it could be a very fruitful one in a local situation.

Prayer and Meditation

The healing ministry must be 'encompassed in prayer', is what I wrote near the beginning of this book.[4] It is wholly true—prayer is power. It is necessary therefore to give some attention to prayer and to remember one of its laws. There is, for example, a spiritual law that the prayer of a group is much more effectual than the individual prayers of its members praying alone. 'Where two or three are gathered together . . .'.[5] It is therefore very important that all present in worship at the time of the ministry should be corporately praying. Such group prayer has an important place in the devotional life of the church.

Contemplative prayer and mysticism—and especially the latter—fall outside the range of the average Christian's spiritual life, although the opportunity to learn about and engage in prayers of contemplation is a blessing indeed. Mysticism is the experience of the few. It is not something which can be created or manufactured. It is a divine gift. We cannot make God choose us for the mystic way.

This is not intended to discourage the development of higher levels of devotion. The way to contemplative prayer is open to all for whom such a privilege is appropriate. My main concern is to stress that we cannot train ourselves to be mystics for the blessing does not come as a result of human effort. What we can do is to embroil ourselves in prayer and devotion so that the mystic way may be opened to us if God so wills.[6]

Meditation is a particular devotional undertaking to which

we can apply ourselves with benefit. I use the word meditation here not in the sense of a spoken address reflecting on a
theme—which is a normal and traditional use—but in the
almost opposite sense of setting aside the rational, intellectual
processes and simply 'being still'. This kind of meditation is
expressed mainly in silence. It is a state of being in which we
open ourselves to the soul within.

In normal life it is the function of the mind to look after all
the practical necessities of life. To be absent-minded in our
kind of world is to live dangerously indeed! There comes the
time of meditation when, being as we must be in a secure
place where the mind does not need to worry about practical
dangers and distractions, it can take its rest and be still.
Meditation, in the way in which I am speaking of it, is in fact
the opposite of thinking. It is the mind at rest. And when the
mind is still, it can begin to know that God *is* God.[7]

In these circumstances, the stilled mind can be, rather than
active in the direction of the world, open to the soul and
especially the apex of the soul in which, in traditional mystic
concepts, the Spirit speaks to our spirit. It is in such a time of
ordered silence that we are in touch with deep-down things.[8]

Meditation periods may be of ten minutes or 60 or whatever time is appropriate. For those experienced in meditation,
the longer the silence and the fewer the words, the better.
Lengthy silence is however a discipline to be learned and both
those new to it and those with a certain kind of temperament
need help with it. In the meditation groups with which I have
been connected we made it our practice to use a theme or a
symbol to help to keep the mind centred on the deep-down
things.[9] This could be a passage of scripture, a particular
symbol—like a rose to look at—or a particular image to which
one could take oneself back if attention wanders. I have
offered meditation outlines in my book *Creative Silence* and
these were so arranged as to be able to be used for twenty
minutes or an hour.[10] The spaces between the words are the
spaces which can be shortened or lengthened according to
need and desire.

Meditation contributes to healing because it is a way of
raising the level of spiritual awareness and it is in these
moments of raised awareness—as the story of the walk to

Emmaus tells us—that 'things happen' for the advancement of our life in the Spirit.[11]

Difficult Areas

There are two areas of real difficulty which ought to be mentioned, although briefly in a book of this kind. One is the area of complementary medicine, and the other is that of spiritualism.

As I noted earlier, I prefer to speak of *complementary* medicine because I have set the whole treatment of this subject in the context of the healing spectrum, the variety of gifts God gives for our wholeness. There are, within the field of the complementary therapies, further gifts for our healing.

I deliberately phrase the position in that way because the so-called alternative or complementary field is so wide and so varied that we must move in it with a degree of responsibility. The field includes what many would see as respectable treatments (for example, homeopathy, osteopathy, acupuncture, reflexology, herbalism, colour healing), that to others are highly fanciful theories. The now common 'mind and body' exhibitions bring together an enormous number of curiosities and so make it impossible to describe the field as a whole as part of God's gifts. It is also complicated by the fact that there are many healing organisations that work from a spiritualist or psychic (in that sense) base.

The result of all this is that, on the medical side, there is a great deal of both suspicion and hostility to practitioners in the complementary treatments. It is, as I said earlier, very difficult for highly trained physicians with very high standards of selection and qualification to take seriously those who offer healing through methods in which very little training is given or supervision required. There are, within the list given above, those with specific and established training schemes, but there are many where little that is called training is required at all. *Spiritual* healing to many medical people simply falls in that area and cannot be taken seriously by them.

Many in the churches also oppose the whole complementary

field and often in their sweeping criticisms classify as occult, satanic, for example, approaches which at least deserve responsible consideration.[12] It seems that wherever the word 'energies' is used, the assumption is made that the approach is of an eastern religious kind and therefore must be 'anti-Christian'. Within this kind of judgment there is often a good deal of misunderstanding, lack of knowledge and of spiritual discernment. The view of man as a complex energy system in which energy channels are blocked and need to be treated does not deserve rejection without understanding. We rightly want to take our stance on a Christ-centred approach—as I have clearly explained[13]—but we have to be careful about dogmatic judgmental and condemnatory attitudes especially where little attempt is made to have knowledge of the full facts.

I would never like to set aside any system just because it spoke in terms of energies, for two reasons. *First*, I do believe that it is, if I understand the message coming from modern physics rightly, in the realm of energy that we need to view life and that great new understanding will come from that area. *Second*, the important point about any energy offered in healing is the *source* of it. Energy is the Greek word *energeia* and that word is used in the New Testament of the Spirit. It is indeed the *energeia* of the Holy Spirit that is needed for health with its total sense of harmony, balance, wholeness. That which needs to be looked at therefore is the source of any energy or energies which we call into the service of helping to promote health. 'Test the spirits' (1 John 4:1, *New International Version*) was the advice. Whatever is of God and good, is God's gift. Whatever is of the energy that is satanic, occult, demonic, reject in the name of Jesus.[14]

There is no subject as likely to divide and disrupt Christians as does any mention of spiritualism. Many totally reject it as of evil—mainly on the basis of a passage in Deuteronomy.[15] I am in no way disposed to make a case for spiritualism. All contact with the negative side of the occult is unhealthy and to be totally avoided. Spiritualism is more likely to lead to disintegration of the personality than to its ultimate benefit. It is often claimed by those who have to minister to those who have been involved in spiritualist approaches to healing that, while immediate physical benefit may occur, the long-term effect on wholeness is unhelpful. That judgment must be taken seriously.

That said, it remains a fact that there are Christian spiritualists who work in the name of Jesus and whose purposes are exactly those represented by the Christian healing ministry. They are people who, like the first disciples, give an impression that 'they have been with Jesus'.[16] The spiritualist way is not one I can recommend. In fact I would always caution against it, but I nevertheless question my right to condemn outright people of Christian, as well as spiritual, integrity who do things in a way of which I cannot see the value or rectitude. So I state my reservations and anxiety about spiritualism and I do not feel it right to minister in that way, but judgment of it—and of those who do it, as of us all—must be left in the hands of God.

What I do feel must be emphasised is the need always to work at the spiritual, and not the psychic (in this sense), level. Too much that takes place in spiritualism is at a level too trivial to fit in with the deep things of God. The whole is a field to be avoided. 'Blessed are those who do not see, yet have believed' said Jesus.[17] The search for proof of survival is an understandable one, but so-called contact with departed spirits at the psychic level is likely to do much more harm than good. The Christian way is the spiritual way, and all our healing ministry must be at that level and not at the psychic level.

I hope I have made my questioning of spiritualism in the healing world clear. All contact with the occult should be avoided. 'Spiritualism is wrong' say the anonymous Two Listeners in the devotional classic *God Calling*—oddly enough often deliberately criticised in evangelical circles as being spiritualist in its content—which is strange indeed![18] That statement represents the biblical and Christian view. To take that position does not and dare not allow us the right of condemnation of Christian spiritualists who claim totally that they are Christ-centred in their ministry. God alone makes that kind of judgment.

Gifts of Healing

I have totally discouraged the use of the word 'healer' in this book on the ground that healing is given by God through the risen Lord, present in Spirit, and that our rôle, unworthy as we are, is that of 'channels' of his peace, his power, and his blessing. This, however, does not exclude the fact that there are, as Paul says so clearly, people with 'gifts of healing'.[19] That he does in fact say some have this gift implies that others do not—as is true of all the gifts he mentions.

Everybody has a healing touch, as the mother, father, grandparent demonstrates to the child with the grazed knee when he/she 'lays hands' on it and says 'There, there, that will make it better'. The potential of touch should never be excluded, in any context. Nevertheless, there are some people with an aptitude as well as an attitude that makes them able to be used in a particular way in the healing ministry. They may sense they are used by God. What is much more important, others may tell them they have such a gift.

Quite often those who have such a healing chrisma have sought to offer it to the church and almost invariably it is rejected. There are, as a result, very good people (there may be some of whom that cannot be said too) who are exercising individual healing ministries outside the church. Often they are bitterly resentful of the church which has rejected them.

Determining whether someone has such a gift or not is extraordinarily difficult and demands a gift of discernment of a high order. Not infrequently—but not, of course, always— people who claim such a gift are unwell, in the sense of balanced and harmonious health, themselves. The reality remains that there are some people with the gift and if it is a gift from God for our healing, it should be given to the church and used, with authority, within the healing community.

It is therefore not only desirable but necessary for churches to set up some structure to deal with this. In some Anglican dioceses, the Bishop will himself decide whether or not to licence a person in this capacity in the diocese or he may ask someone who has experience and authority in the field to make a recommendation on the person concerned. In other churches, variants on this process of 'testing' a gift have been considered. My own church, the Church of Scotland, has suggested that each Presbytery set up an informal panel which would include a member of the medical profession to deal with requests to be so recognised and used. The end result is a good one for:

a   the ministry takes place in the name of the church and from within it as one of the healing ministries it can offer;
b   the person ministering goes 'in the name of the Church' and is affirmed because of that;
c   the person to whom ministry is given has some sense of confidence in that the ministry has been given authority.

The testing of a healing gift must be much more in the character and gifts of an applicant than in any question of physical successes. Whether the ministrant-to-be presents appropriate humility rather than inappropriate arrogance, has motives encompassed in self-giving rather than receiving, is seen to be one who has been with Jesus, are the kind of areas that lead to decision. The number of people who will minister in this way is smaller rather than greater, but there can be no doubt of the existence of such gifted people. They can bring great blessing and in so conveying blessing in Jesus' name, they will themselves be blessed.

Another area for enquiry is the relationship of money to healing. While those who give their whole time, their property and themselves to a healing function must have a right to support themselves through their work ('the labourer *is* worthy of his hire', Luke 10:7, *Authorised Version*), any attitude which puts emphasis on financial return as such must be suspect.

Anointing

Anointing is based on James 5:13–16 and is a practice followed in some traditions. The marking of the sign of the cross in oil on the forehead, a biblical symbol of healing, is found by many who receive it to be a means of grace. It is, as distinct from laying on of hands which is properly repeated many times as we move along the road to wholeness, usually carried out on a specific occasion. The practice is biblical and so carries that authority.

There are many other questions of detail arising from the matters discussed in this contribution to the literature on healing ministry and to the area of pastoral study. What remains important are the biblical grounds on which the whole approach is based. The reason for the healing ministry is that Jesus commanded it as a complement to preaching with boldness. To heal the sick or play any tiny part in ministry to that end in Jesus' name, is the greatest privilege in the world. It must bring an attitude of praise and thanksgiving, and the element of thanksgiving must always play a prominent part in healing services. And if, as we believe, the laying on of hands is not merely a liturgical symbol but a conveying of power, that power is given as God's gift for our health and healing. And as for the first disciples the signs and wonders will be a demonstration of that message which the miracle in the book of Acts conveyed to all. Those involved in the ministry were all filled with the Holy Spirit. So must the church, the healing community, be filled. So must we all.

Notes to Chapter 12

1   Howard Booth, *Healing Is Wholeness*, available through all book-shops, ISBN 0 951 2420 8 or direct (plus post and packing) from The Division of Social Responsibility of the Methodist Church, 1 Central Buildings, London SW1H 9NH, or from CCHH, St Marylebone Parish Church, Marylebone Road, London NW1 5LT.
2   This will include cassette tapes and videos.
3   Produced by CCHH (see note 1 above for an address).
4   On page 14.
5   Matthew 18:20
6   The case of Simon Magus whom I mentioned earlier in the discussion and who tried to buy the Holy Spirit is indeed a cautionary tale in this field—Acts, chapter 8, verses 9–24.
7   Psalm 46:10
8   A phrase from Gerard Manley Hopkins poem *The Grandeur of God* from *Selected Poems* (Heinemann, 1953).
9   These groups were mainly led by my friend Martin Israel, the noted spiritual writer, pathologist, priest and mystic.

10 Denis Duncan, *Creative Silence* (Arthur James, 1980).
11 Luke 24:13–35
12 The writings of Roy Livesey on this subject are an example of an uncritical approach of this kind.
13 See page 110.
14 Discernment is a *very* important gift and must be cultivated.
15 Deuteronomy 18:11
16 Acts 4:13
17 John 20:29
18 *God Calling* (Arthur James), *God at Eventide* (Arthur James).
19 I Corinthians 12:9

13

The Way Ahead

Within the last decade the whole area of health and healing has changed significantly. The movement back to the Christian healing ministry and the degree of recovery of that ministry has, as I have argued in the early part of this book, had an exhilarating effect in all the churches. In that area a victory has been won. It is, as yet, not accurate to say that the healing ministry is now seen as a normal part of the church's witness and service, but it is possible to say that no church as a body or any of its clergy individually can be unaware of the impact that ministry is having.

This does not, of course, mean that the church as a whole, or its individual servants, are *all* convinced that the church should express such a ministry in the ways I have now described. There are many who, on theological grounds, want to know much more about the ministry before they involve themselves or their church in it. There are others who have been adversely affected by particular approaches to healing which they find unacceptable, offensive, ill-balanced, even dangerous.[1] Because phrases like 'the ministry of healing' suggest public hysterical occasions to them, they want none of it. There are those who are, for various reasons, positively opposed to this ministry. I would myself expect a wave of quite hostile reaction, theologically and in other ways, against the healing ministry in the not-too-distant future. A testing time for the ministry lies ahead, I believe, and sooner rather than later. This need not be a worry. To be attacked is often to be strengthened. We must constantly examine our commitment to this ministry and, it may be, adjust our practices. In this field in which human fears and hopes, anxieties and expectations are at the very centre of the issue, responsible care and informed self-criticism, under God, are essential elements in the process that is evolving, a process that will be to the glory of God.

As in so many other fields, the development of the concepts of health and healing dare not stand still. If they do, they will stagnate. The implications of the call to heal the sick must, as I have suggested earlier in this book, always include corporate aspects of healing. I take the phrase directly from the late and influential doctor-theologian R A (Bob) Lambourne, who made it the sub-title of his important book, *Community, Church and Healing*, already mentioned.[2]

The emphasis on corporate Christianity is spread through the vocabulary of the New Testament. Church, fellowship, community, body of Christ, the Kingdom of God—so many words speak of that inter-relationship between people, expressed in bonds of many kinds. No man or woman is an island.[3] Whatever emphasis there is in the Bible on the necessity of individual conversion, commitment and faith, the results are always to be expressed in corporate fellowship and mutual love.

The New Testament builds on the Old Testament, Christianity builds on Judaism, the church is a New Testament organism as was the people of God. The Christian Gospel could do nothing other than express itself through a community of people, fired by a common enthusiasm, bound together by a common loyalty and growing together in the knowledge and power of its Lord. It is therefore the healing community with a responsibility for the health of its members and with an obligation to offer health and wholeness to those outside it, too.

That offer is one made to individuals but it is also one made in relation to corporate bodies. Christians are called to be 'ministers of reconciliation' and the church is commanded to offer 'a ministry of reconciliation'.[4] It must take its healing ministry into the community, local, national and international. It must engage in the healing of the nations.[5] It must be involved in the increasing divisions in society. It must recognise that the multi-racial society is a reality of our present and future. The healing of divisions fuelled for inter-racial dis-ease is a prime obligation on those who believe in the healing way. The world is now a global village. The financial crises of one nation bring about a world chain re-action that affects many more, if not every other country. In a world made one through technology on the ground and in the atmosphere, there must be a constant and deliberate effort to heal division and create community. The full impact of the pressure to take the healing ministry 'into all the world'—in various contemporary understandings of that phrase—will be strongly present in the next decade. There is a health the world needs. There are the forces of healing available to it if the determination to find and to use them is present.

It is essential, however, that the body called to heal the nations as well as individuals and bring them towards health and wholeness, realises that healing must begin within the church itself. Jesus, in his teaching the disciples about unity and fellowship, stressed the need to be one 'that the world may believe'.[6] Unity is clearly linked to evangelism. The Spirit brings not disorder but order (and this is always a relevant test of the presence of the Spirit in any undertaking), of integration not disintegration. The church cannot live easily with 'the shattered cross'.[7] Its ethos is expressed in community and its faith is founded on communion. The way ahead for the healing ministry will be demanding but, where it is seen to be evidence of the Gospel in words and action, it will have profound effects.

It has been made clear to me beyond doubt—and I think of situations I know, where the ministry has been introduced and developed through prayer, biblical study, worship expressed in blessing by laying on of hands—that the spiritual level of a congregation's or parish's life has been notably heightened.

The recovery of the healing ministry and the effort to understand all that it means, is not to be the undertaking of a group or clique on the fringe of a church's life. It is taking seriously the fundamental obligations of the Gospel and applying them with boldness and in compassion for the bless-ing of people and the glory of God.

The way to health through healing is the way of the Lord who was moved to compassion by the needs of those whom he encountered as he went about doing good. The disciple must be as his or her master.[8]

To sustain and develop the healing ministry, there remains a theological task that must be undertaken now. The healing ministry has not had, up to the time of writing, the extended attention of major academic theologians. The number of books on healing, healing ministry, health and wholeness is now large but none tackles, head-on, the theological foundations of this kind of ministry. We cannot allow the literature of the healing ministry to be no more than a welter of anecdotes, however moving and impressive, nor leave it to any one theological approach, especially if extreme, to claim the central ground for its own.

This book is not anecdotal. Case illustrations have been deliberately avoided for, even though names can be changed and so on, it is all too easy, through links and associations, to discover whose story is being told and confidentiality does not allow that to happen. It has however been written in a popular, rather than an academic, way to fulfil the purpose laid down for it. The major theological work needed is still to be published. It lies far beyond the competence of this author to do it. I hope however that this work is barely in the bookshops before the groundwork is beginning to be done in making possible a setting out of the theological grounds which make it obligatory that Christians should not hold back from, in the fullest sense, preaching the Gospel and healing the sick in the power of Jesus' name, and through every gift that has been given.

The great doctrines of our faith—the Incarnation, the Resurrection, the gift of the Spirit, forgiveness, grace, salvation—all undergird the theme and practice of the healing ministry. The nature of the healing way is shaped by those beliefs. The way ahead for the healing ministry will be determined by a greater understanding of these foundation doctrines of our faith. May God raise up now those who can help the church to understand its faith more completely and, in so doing, make clear that the miracles, signs, wonders—the divine surprises—that are evidence of the presence and power of the Kingdom will, however they come and through whatever disciplines they are expressed, bring health and healing to the world and its people.

Notes to Chapter 13

1   A young mother in a wheel-chair, a nurse by profession, complained bitterly to me about so many people making naïve suggestions about prayer, healing and faith to her. This she had found offensive, given her condition—multiple sclerosis, with which she had to live.

2   R A Lambourne, *Community, Church and Healing*, new edition (Arthur James, 1987).

3   John Donne, *Devotions upon Emergent Occasions*.

4   II Corinthians 5:18

5   This was, in fact, the title of the 1985 Annual Lecture of The Churches' Council for Health and Healing. It was given by Kenneth Greet.

6   John 17:21

7   This expression was the title of a famous little book of yesteryear on disunity and division by T H Robinson.

8   Matthew 10:25

Resources Appendix

There are many resources available to those interested in the study of health and healing ministry. The main one in terms of the approach of this book to the subject and the working out of it in the practical life of the Church, is:

The Churches' Council for Health and Healing
St Marylebone Parish Church
Marylebone Road
London NW1 5LT
Tel: 01–486 9644 (24hr answering service)

These resources are in the following areas:

1 *Literature:*
   CCHH publications and other books listed on CCHH Supplements which can be obtained free from the above address.
2 *Cassette tapes:* They include:
   Dr Chris Andrews (1986–87)—The Healing of the Memories
   Howard Booth—The Church, The Healing Community
   Bill Burridge—Anxiety, Stress and Relaxation
   Christopher Hamel Cooke—Healing & Counselling, The St Marylebone Model
   —The Casework Relationship: A Christian Perspective
   —Creation: The Evaluation of Prayer and The Healing of Expectations
   —The Healing Sacraments
   Dr Tony Dale (1985–86)—The Healing of the Memories
   Denis Duncan—The Christian Healing Ministry Today
   —Whole Person Ministry
   —Miracle and The Mystery of Suffering
   —The Unconscious

Dr Martin Israel—The Inner Life of the Counsellor
Benita Kyle—Healing Relationships: Everyday Relationships
—Healing Relationships: Counselling Relationships
Richard McLaren—The Spirituality of the Counsellor
Bishop Morris Maddocks—Theological Bases of Healing
Edwin Robertson—Biblical Bases of Healing
John Schild—Prayer and Prayer Groups
—The Laying on of Hands
Dr Janet Seregeant—An ABC of Mental Illness
Sheila Smith—Bereavement I and II (2 tapes)
Renata Symonds—Dreams

3 *Videos:* Denis Duncan—The Healing Ministry
There are two videos, one lasting 46.50 minutes (VHS and Betamax), and the other in VHS only reduced to 36 minutes. Both are available for sale or hire from the CCHH office. The presentation follows the approach of this volume.

A short video, useful for training purposes is available from The Acorn Trust, Whitehill Chase, Bordon, Hampshire.

4 *Books:* Since there is a large number of books on both health and healing, the list given below is a selection from the bibliographies available from the CCHH at the address given above.

J P Baker, *Salvation and Wholeness: The Biblical Perspective of Healing* (Fountain Trust, London 1973)
This small book is a handy and concise presentation of the Biblical understanding of health and healing in terms of the Bible's teaching about men and salvation. It includes a consideration of the occurrence of miracles of healing in Biblical times and today.

George Bennett, *The Heart of Healing* (Arthur James, London)
The ministry of George Bennett at Crowhurst in Sussex has been a focal point in practical healing ministry.

Howard Booth, *In Search of Health and Wholeness.* (Division of Social Responsibility of the Methodist Church, 1985).
A workbook for individual and group study.

Howard Booth, *Healing Experiences* (Bible Reading Fellowship, 1986).
A devotional guide for personal study.

Howard Booth. *Healing IS Wholeness*, (Division of Social Responsibility of the Methodist Church with CCHH, 1987).

A resource book on health and healing.

Michael Botting, *Christian Healing in the Parish* (Grove Books, Bramcote, Nottingham 1977).

An outline treatment of the subject beginning with the Bible and ending with suggestions about how the ministry of healing may be practised in the parish today.

Christopher Hamel Cooke, *Health is for God*, (Arthur James, 1986)

The Rector of St Marylebone Parish Church writes from a sacramental view of healing, and deals with matters related to that approach. He particularly expresses the doctrine of (continuing) Creation as a basis for an understanding of healing.

Denis Duncan, *Creative Silence* (Arthur James, London 1980)

A book in which the author takes into consideration 'the unconscious' in dis-ease and healing.

Denis Duncan, *Love, the Word that heals*, (Arthur James, 1981)

An exposition of I Corinthians 13 (the William Barclay version as in *The New Testament, A Translation by William Barclay*) (Arthur James, 1988).

V Edmunds and C G Scorer, *Some Thoughts on Faith Healing* (Christian Medical Fellowship, London 1979)

This is the record of an enquiry into 'faith healing' made by a study group of Christian doctors. It considers the Biblical basis of healing and the gifts of healing, and traces the history of 'faith-healing' in the church. It is a very thorough study within its limits and concludes with a consideration of the situation today.

Monica Furlong, *Burrswood: Focus on Healing* (Hodder & Stoughton)

An assessment of the great healing ministry at Burrswood, which was founded by Dorothy Kerin.

P L Garlick, *Man's Search for Health: A Study in the Interrelation of Religion and Medicine* (Highway Press, London 1952)

Miss Garlick provides a broad historical view of healing in both religion and medicine in Europe, Africa and Asia. She sets forth the basis of the Church's healing ministry and describes the contribution of the modern missionary movement of the western church. She concludes by suggesting how the healing work of the church and medicine can find a new synthesis in the idea of wholeness.

Jean C Grigor, *Loss—An invitation to grow* (Arthur James, 1986)

The opportunity for growth towards wholeness through suffering is developed by an experienced pastoral counsellor.

John Gunstone, *The Lord is our Healer*, (Hodder and Stoughton, 1986)

A 'charismatic' approach on the theme of the relevance of renewal in the Holy Spirit to the Church's ministry of healing.

Martin Israel, *The Pain that Heals* (Hodder & Stoughton)

A study of suffering and its creative potential by a distinguished pathologist and mystic.

Morton Kelsey, *Healing and Christianity in Ancient Thought and Modern Times* (SCM Press, London 1973)

This study is concerned with religious or sacramental healing and traces its history from Biblical times to the present. It ends with a plea for the recognition of the importance of religious healing so that it is given a place in theology and in the life of the church. Presently out of print.

R A Lambourne, *Community, Church and Healing: A study of some of the corporate aspects of the Church's ministry to the sick* (Arthur James, 1987)

The late Dr Lambourne, who was a psychiatrist, emphasises the church's corporate healing ministry as manifested particularly through the life and worship of the Christian congregation. It relates medical and theological thinking and has interesting and pertinent suggestions to make.

C S Lewis, *A Grief Observed* (Faber and Faber)

One of the most moving and helpful books in the field of bereavement.

Francis MacNutt, *Healing* (Ave Maria Press, Notre Dame, Indiana 1974)

Francis MacNutt is a Roman Catholic priest who was influenced by Agnes Sanford and practised an active healing ministry in America. This was his first book on the subject and is written in a lively style. He recognises three basic kinds of sickness—spiritual, emotional and physical—and describes four prayer methods by which these might be healed.

Morris Maddocks, *The Christian Healing Ministry* (SPCK, London 1981)

This book is 'an eloquent defence of healing in an orthodox Christian context'. It takes a broad view of healing as including both medical and non-medical types, and deals with the subject in three parts. First—Health and the Kingdom of God (as set out in the New Testament); second—Healing in the (Modern) Church; third—Health and Society.

Morris Maddocks, *Journey towards Wholeness* (SPCK, 1986)

Ian Pearce, *The Gate of Healing* (Neville Spearman)

An exposition especially related to the study of cancer.

J Cameron Peddie, *The Forgotten Talent* (Arthur James, 1985)

Written in the fifties by 'the saint of the Gorbals', Cameron Peddie's book is a basic plea for the recovery of the Healing Ministry. Mr Peddie had a healing sanctuary in the Gorbals district of Glasgow and was responsible for leading many involved in the ministry today towards it.

William Portsmouth, *Healing Prayer* (Arthur James, London)

A helpful devotional book, specifically relating prayer and healing.

John Richards, *But Deliver us from Evil—An Introduction to the Demonic Dimension in Pastoral Care* (Darton, Longman and Todd, London 1974)

In this book Mr Richards, an Anglican priest, begins with an account of healing in the modern Church and then passes to the phenomenon of the occult in the world today, including the problem of demon possession. This is followed by a discussion on how men and women may find in Jesus Christ deliverance from bondage to demons including, where required, their exorcism.

There is also a useful booklet by Mr Richards entitled *Exorcism, Deliverance and Healing* (Grove Books, Bramcote, Nottingham 1976)

It considers the modern understanding of exorcism as set out in recent church reports, together with practical guidelines and forms of service for use in a pastoral situation.

Louis Rose, *Faith Healing* (Penguin, Harmondsworth 1971)

An interesting study of 'faith-healing' by a psychiatrist. The approach is historical and the book ends with an attempt to investigate and evaluate modern activity. Useful for background reading, but regards faith-healing as opposed to what the author calls 'scientific healing'

Agnes Sanford, *The Healing Light* (Arthur James, London 1949),

A much re-reprinted and popular account of Mrs Sanford's experience as a spiritual healer in the USA. In this book she 'shows how to get God's Healing Power flowing through us and gives illustrations of real people whom she has known who have passed from pain and cynicism to health and abounding joy'.

Agnes Sanford, *Healing Gifts of the Spirit* (Arthur James, London)

Mrs Sanford was one of the most highly respected and widely read channels of healing ministry. Her books are in the 'popular' category.

C G Scorer, *Healing: Biblical, Medical and Pastoral* (Christian Medical Fellowship, London 1979)

A Christian surgeon writes a brief outline of healing as seen from Biblical, medical and pastoral points of view. By 'pastoral healing', is meant healing in a church context today. He concludes with a brief critical evaluation of the idea of the ministry of healing of the Church, which he distinguishes from medical healing, but makes a plea for co-operation between the two.

Paul Tournier, *A Doctor's Casebook in the light of the Bible* (SCM).

United Presbyterian Church in the USA *The Relation of Christian Faith to Health* (UPC, Philadelphia 1960)

This was the Report to the 1960 General Assembly of the

United Presbyterian Church in the USA of a special committee on this subject set up in 1956 by that Church. It is the most useful of several Reports produced by the major denominations of the Christian church.

Saxon Walker, *Sheila—A healing through dying* (Arthur James, 1987)

The story of Sheila's last year by her priest husband, and the way in which both grew towards wholeness through the experience of her dying.

Leslie Weatherhead, *Psychology, Religion and Healing*

A classic in the field of a pioneer in healing ministry. Out of print at present.

John Wilkinson, *Health and Healing: Studies in New Testament Principles and Practice* (Handsel Press, Edinburgh 1980)

This book is a study of the Biblical understanding of health and healing. It begins with a consideration of what the Old and New Testaments mean by health and this is followed by an examination of healing in the New Testament. It combines both medical and theological insight and ends with a discussion of the ministry of healing in the church today in the light of New Testament principles and practice.

Dr Wilkinson, both medical and ordained, is noted for his Bible studies in this field.

Michael Wilson, *The Church is Healing* (SCM Press, London 1966)

Dr Wilson seeks to define the church and healing. He speaks of the church gathered for healing as a congregation and the church scattered as its members in the healing professions. He details the healing activities of the congregation and their relation to the world of medicine. The book concludes with a consideration of the ways forward in co-operation.

5 *A Healing Kit:*

The United Reformed Church has produced a healing kit of great value for any church seeking to develop a healing ministry. It is available from the URC Health and Healing Committee, 86 Tavistock Place, London WC1R 9HT.

The URC has also produced a filmstrip—Christian Healing in the local Church. It is available from the same address.

6 *National Christian Healing Organisations*:
Burrswood Home of Healing, Groombridge, nr Tunbridge Wells, Kent TN3 9PY – Tel: 089 286 3637
The Churches' Council for Health and Healing, St Marylebone Parish Church, Marylebone Road, London NW1 5LT – Tel: 01–486 9644
The Christian Medical Commission, The World Council of Churches, 150 route de Fernay, 1211 Geneva, Switzerland
The Divine Healing Mission, The Old Rectory, Crowhurst, nr Battle, East Sussex TN33 9AD – Tel: 042 483 204
The Guild of Health, Edward Wilson House, 26 Queen Anne Street, London W1 – Tel: 01–580 2492
The Guild of St Raphael, St Marylebone Parish Church, Marylebone Road, London NW1 5LT – Tel: 01–935 6374
The Order of St Luke the Physician, St Marylebone Parish Church, Marylebone Road, London NW1 5LT – Tel: 01–935 6374
The Scottish Christian Fellowship of Healing, Holy Corner Church Centre, 15 Morningside Road, Edinburgh EH10 4DP – Tel: 031–447 9383

7 *Residential Homes of Healing:*
Each Healing home has its own particular emphasis. It is advisable to contact the home for full details before making a booking. Please also note that new homes are constantly opening. A full list with additional details can be obtained from CCHH at the address given earlier.
Burrswood, Groombridge, Tunbridge Wells, Kent TN3 9PY – Tel: 0892 86 3637
Christ Home, 21 Queen's Parade, Cleethorpes, South Humberside DN35 0DF – Tel: 0472 696548
Crowhurst, The Old Rectory, Crowhurst, near Battle, East Sussex TN33 9AD – Tel: 042 483 204
Friends Fellowship of Healing, Claridge House, Dormansland, Lingfield, Surrey RH7 6QH – Tel: 0342 832150
Friends Fellowship of Healing, Lattendales, Greystoke, Penrith, Cumbria CA11 0UE – Tel: 08533 229
Green Pastures, 17 Burton Road, Branksome Park, Bournemouth BH13 6DT – Tel: 0202 764776
The Old Bakery, Hindolveston, Dereham, Norfolk NR20 5DF – Tel: 0263 861325

Resthaven Home of Healing Ltd, Pitchcombe, near Stroud, Gloucestershire GL6 6LS – Tel: 0452 812682
St Julian's, Coolham, near Horsham, West Sussex RH13 8QL – Tel: 040 387 220
Spennithorne, near Leyburn, North Yorkshire DL8 5PR – Tel: 0969 23233

Final note: it is particularly stressed that the Resources area in Health and Healing is changing all the time. The information given above is a selection. For further details and information please contact CCHH.